FIRESIDE

By the same authors
The Pow! Zap! Wham! Comic Book Trivia Quiz

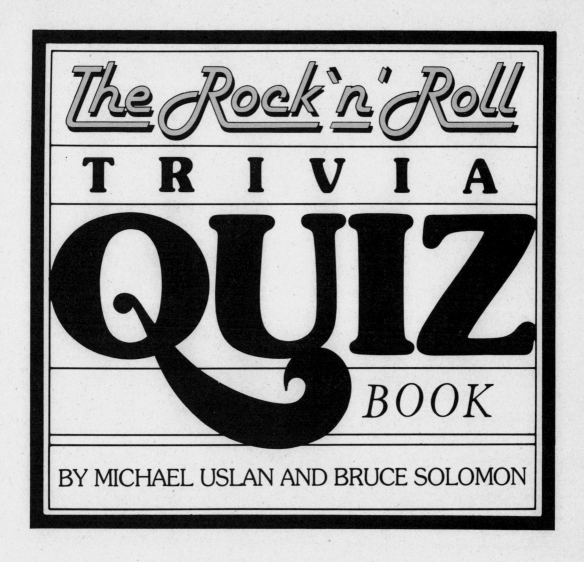

The Rock 'n' Roll
TRIVIA
QUIZ
BOOK

BY MICHAEL USLAN AND BRUCE SOLOMON

Designed by Joel Avirom

A FIRESIDE BOOK
Published by Simon and Schuster

A Fireside Book
Published by Simon and Schuster
A Division of Gulf & Western Corporation
Simon & Schuster Building
Rockefeller Center
1230 Avenue of the Americas
New York, New York 10020

Manufactured in the United States of America

1 2 3 4 5 6 7 8 9 10

Library of Congress Cataloging in Publication Data

Uslan, Michael, date.
    The rock 'n' roll trivia quiz book.
    (A Fireside book)
    1. Rock music—Miscellanea.   I. Solomon, Bruce, joint
author.   II. Title.
ML3545.U8   784   78-13037

ISBN 0-671-24264-4

This is dedicated
to the one I love —
xxxx

Contents

Contents

For the Record

From the beginnings of rock 'n' roll in 1955, right up to the present, there have been a number of individuals who have contributed something special and unique to the music-personality. These people have given an identity to the music of the younger half of the population. Growing up in the New York metropolitan area, we were raised and later nurtured by the golden throats of disc jockeys like Alan Freed, Murray the K, B. Mitchell Reed, the WMCA Good Guys, Gus Gossard, Scott Muni, Zacherle, Jim Lowe, Cousin Brucie Morrow, Dick Heatherton, and Don Imus. A generation tips its collective hat to you all.

The authors would like to thank the people who contributed to their own disc-jockey days: Terry Abler, who gave Bruce his first pro DJ job on WYXE–FM, Madison, Wisconsin; Bill Cross, Bruce's roommate, who co-hosted his oldies show, "Give Grease a Chance"; Historical Howard Landsman, who created the oldies show; Dr. Larry Hoffman, who co-created the oldies show "Bloomington Bandstand" with Michael on WIUS, Bloomington, Indiana; Marc Caplan, co-host of "Bloomington Bandstand" for two years after Larry moved on to dental school, cohort in running all the Indiana University sock hops, and co-producer of the TV pilot "At the Hop"; and the rest of the Bandstand gang: Ken MacManus, Frankie B. Rhoads, Sterno, Bubbles Heckman, RoseAnn, Nancy and all the Trivia Hot-Line Girls, Jerry Mishkin, and Denny Thomas.

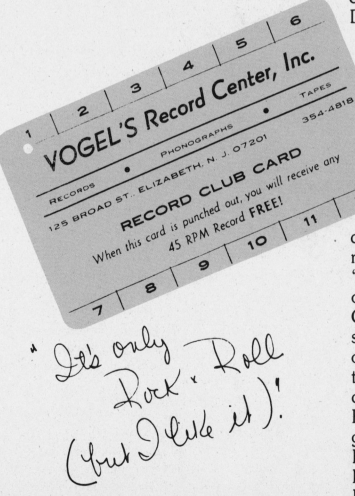

VOGEL'S Record Center, Inc.

RECORDS · PHONOGRAPHS · TAPES

125 BROAD ST., ELIZABETH, N.J. 07201 · 354-4818

RECORD CLUB CARD

When this card is punched out, you will receive any 45 RPM Record FREE!

1 2 3 4 5 6 7 8 9 10 11 12

"It's only Rock & Roll (but I Like it)!"

Cousin Brucie by Michael Uslan

In the spinning world of rock 'n' roll radio (which is known for continual change and as many as forty-five revolutions per minute), perhaps the most well known voice of the past twenty years has belonged to New York disc jockey Cousin Brucie Morrow. He is perhaps the most authoritative man in the radio industry and the perfect one to cowrite this volume with. However, the Cousin Brucie I did cowrite this book with is merely my very own Cousin Brucie Solomon from Roselle, New Jersey.

What does he know about rock 'n' roll? Everything! Bruce was raised on the 45-rpm collections of Dr. Paul C. Uslan of Ann Arbor, Michigan (who introduced him to such immortal tunes as "Rip Van Winkle"), and Dr. Paul E. Hyman of Bayonne, New Jersey (who raised him on "Unchained Melody" by Vito and the Salutations, among other classics). From that early training, it was only natural that Bruce would become a highly rated oldies disc jockey for WYXE–FM in Madison, Wisconsin, and add to his music experience by spinning stacks of wax at local bars and becoming the leader of the original Bruce and the Boulevards.

As captain of his college trivia team, he led his protégés to victory three out of three years at the University of Wisconsin. He furthered his trivia skill by co-authoring the book *The Pow! Zap! Wham! Comic Book Trivia Quiz.*

Bruce grew up on Belmont Avenue in Jersey City and always wanted to join Dion and the Belmonts as a wailer. He has since settled for being an attorney in the entertainment field. His sister, Lisa, is disgusted.

Cousin Michael by Bruce Solomon

One of Michael Uslan's earliest recollections is sitting in front of the family television each afternoon of his preschool days and watching helplessly as his older brother Paul came home from school, flipped off "Officer Joe and the Three Stooges," and turned on "American Bandstand." Day in and day out it was the same thing. When rock 'n' roll wasn't blaring from the shows of Dick Clark, Clay Cole, or Lloyd Thaxton, the old Victrola would be spinning out the melodies of the Platters or the Duprees. Obviously, some of this music had to sink in and leave an eternal imprint on the young lad's mind. I asked Michael about this recently, and he replied, "Sha na na na na na na na na oh yip yip yip yip yip yip yip yip boom boom boom boom boom boom."

The scene shifts to Indiana University, 1970. Michael takes his collection of over one thousand forty-fives (permanently "borrowed" from his brother Paul) and, with the help of a fraternity brother, creates a free-form 1950's oldies show called "Bloomington Bandstand." The success of the radio show led Michael to running sock hops and putting together a Bloomington Bandstand lip synch and dance group that rode motorcycles, dressed in black leather and appeared at campus parties. A representative for an Indianapolis station saw the show and had Michael and the gang write and produce a one-shot TV show on the 1950's . . . over a year before *Happy Days*.

Michael is currently an attorney in charge of motion pictures for United Artists and one day hopes to decipher all the words of "Louie, Louie."

Introduction: "Rock 'n' Roll Is Here to Stay!"

It's true, you know. When it first emerged in 1955, rock 'n' roll was banned by terrified town councils, reviled by clergymen, and purged by parents and teachers. Today, it is twenty-three years old. Sure it has developed, matured, sometimes regressed, but it keeps changing. Rock 'n' roll was born from rhythm and blues plus rockabilly. It went from the hard-core rock of Bill Haley and the Comets to the soft-core roll of Frankie Avalon. It endured the onslaught of the British sound and split off into the direction of soul. It survived the bubble-gum sound and

evolved into acid rock. Today, rock 'n' roll is a mixture of all the above. Though it often seems directionless, as if waiting for a messiah to plot a new course, as the Beatles and Elvis once did, the music is still vibrant and remains the calling card of the latest generation.

Now let's have some nostalgic fun with rock 'n' roll. In this book, we'll cover the songs and singers of 1955–1977. No matter whether your favorite stars were Chuck Berry, Little Anthony and the Imperials, Connie Francis, Gerry and the Pacemakers, the Four Seasons, the Supremes, the Rolling Stones, Tom Jones, Del Shannon, Buddy Holly, the Doors, Jimi Hendrix, Peter, Paul and Mary, Elton John, Sonny and

Cher, or Bruce Springsteen, you'll find your musical era well represented in these pages.

Trivia—the game of instant recall, where the names of stars, groups, songs, and labels suddenly become valuable answers instead of useless information. What was the name of Elvis Presley's back-up group? Who sang "Runaround Sue"? In "Love Potion No. 9," on what street corner did the singer kiss a cop? How many times was the widow next door married in "I'm Henry VIII"? What did K.C. and the Sunshine Band tell you to shake? How much did you remember? The answers lie within. Play the newest oldest game in the country—Trivia!

Rock'n'Roll is Here to Stay!

Let's go back!
  Back to the days when grease was more than the drippings off a pizza,
  But was a way of life;
  When White Socks were more than a baseball team,
  But were the coolest way to dress;
  When White Bucks meant more than Buck Owens and Buck Henry,
  But were the neatest shoes in town;
  When bleeding madras was more than a leaky waterbed,
  But were the swiftest shirts around;
  And when man's best friend was his comb.
It was the 1950's to early 60's.
It was the first years of Rock 'n' Roll.

Quizzes

ONCE IS NOT ENOUGH!

Sometimes in the world of rock 'n' roll, a singer or a group will have so much success with one song that they will record it again. Of course, they might find it hard to sell the same song over and over to the same people, so they change the beat a little here and tinker with the words there. And—voila!—a "new" song. Award yourself one point for each follow-up song you identify correctly.

QUESTION		POINTS
1.	The Beach Boys had their first big hit in 1962 with "Surfin' Safari." It took them a year to have a second hit. It was:	
	a. Surf City	
	b. Surfin' USA	
	c. Surfer Girl	
	d. Help Me, Rhonda	
	e. I've Got to Hire a New Record Promoter	
2.	Diane Renay's follow-up to "Navy Blue" was the unforgettable:	
	a. Khaki Green	
	b. Soldier Boy	
	c. I'm Joining the WAVES	
	d. Kiss Me, Sailor	
	e. Seasick on a Submarine	
3.	The Marcels did irreparable harm to the music and lyrics of Rodgers and Hart with their stirring rendition of "Blue Moon" in 1961. What song did they irreparably harm next?	
	a. Heartaches	
	b. Heart and Soul	
	c. My Heart Stood Still	
	d. Rain in My Heart	
	e. Rodgers and Hart Transplant	

ONCE IS NOT ENOUGH!

QUESTION		POINTS
4.	The Happenings did to George and Ira Gershwin with "I Got Rhythm" what the Marcels did to Rodgers and Hart with "Blue Moon." What was the Happenings' follow-up record?	
	a. Summertime	
	b. Old Man River	
	c. Smoke Gets in Your Eyes	
	d. See You in September	
	e. My Mammy	
5.	The Four Tops scored big with "I Can't Help Myself (Sugar Pie, Honey Bunch)." Then they recorded the same song, changing the lyrics to protect the innocent. This song was:	
	a. The Same Old Song	
	b. Baby, I Need Your Lovin'	
	c. Bernadette	
	d. Shake Me, Wake Me	
	e. Sugar Pie, Honey Bunch (I Can't Help Myself)	
6.	Lesley Gore wailed "It's My Party" all the way to the Top Ten in 1963. What song did she wail up the charts next?	
	a. The Party's Over	
	b. I Don't Want to Spoil the Party	
	c. Party Lights	
	d. Judy's Turn to Cry	
	e. Next Week the Party's at Your House	
7.	George McCrae had a number-one song in 1974 in "Rock your Baby." His wife Gwen had the follow-up hit in 1975. It was:	
	a. Rock the Boat	
	b. You're Having my Baby	
	c. Rockin' Chair	
	d. Love to Love You, Baby	
	e. Keepin' It in the Family	

ONCE IS NOT ENOUGH!

QUESTION		POINTS
8.	Chubby Checker had one of the biggest hits of the 1960's with "The Twist." What did he do after "The Twist"?	
	a. Twistin' USA	
	b. Let's Twist Again	
	c. Peppermint Twist	
	d. The Pony	
	e. A Visit to the Chiropractor	
9.	After the Drifters went "Under the Boardwalk," their next single was:	
	a. Up on the Roof	
	b. On Broadway	
	c. Saturday Night at the Movies	
	d. I've Got Sand in my Shoes	
	e. In Jail on a Morals Charge	
10.	Harry Nilsson received a gold record for his album satirically titled *Nilsson Schmilsson*. What did he call his next album?	
	a. *Nilsson Schmilsson, Volume 2*	
	b. *More Nilsson Schmilsson*	
	c. *Nilsson Schmilsson, Nilsson Schmilsson*	
	d. *Son of Schmilsson*	
	e. *The Return of Schmilsson*	
11.	Dobie Gray was in with "The In Crowd" in 1965. It took him nine years to be in with the record-buying public again. Dobie's 1974 hit was:	
	a. The Out Crowd	
	b. Seasons in the Sun	
	c. Drift Away	
	d. It's Been a Long, Long Time	
	e. Overnight Sensation	

ONCE IS NOT ENOUGH!

QUESTION		POINTS
12.	Claude King had a hit record in the early 60's called "Wolverton Mountain." It was answered by a song entitled "I'm the Girl on Wolverton Mountain." Who sang this tender refrain?	
	a. Elly Mae Clampett	
	b. Bea Benadaret	
	c. Brenda Lee	
	d. Rosalynn Carter	
	e. Jo Ann Campbell	
	Total Points:	

On the Street Where You Live!

There have been many records singing the praises of highways, byways, streets, avenues, boulevards, and dirt paths. Unfold your map of rock 'n' roll and identify the artist who popularized each street in song. Each is worth one point.

13. Abbey Road _____

14. South Street _____

15. On Broadway _____

16. Boogaloo Down Broadway _____

17. Funky Broadway _____

18. Nights on Broadway _____

19. Second Avenue _____

20. Creeque Alley _____

21. Tobacco Road _____

22. Dead End Street _____

23. Love Street _____

24. Positively Fourth Street _____

25. Penny Lane _____

26. Dancing in the Street _____

27. Take Me Home, Country Roads _____

28. The Long and Winding Road _____

29. The 59th Street Bridge Song (Feeling Groovy) _____

Points: _____

For one point each list the artists who made these "Woman"-titled songs famous hits.

A Woman's Place is in the Song!

30.	31.
Girl, You'll be a Woman Soon	I Got a Woman

32.	33.
Woman, Woman	(Slow Down) Sweet Talkin' Woman

34.	35.	36.	37.
She's a Woman	Evil Woman Don't Play Your Games with Me	Black Magic Woman	Boogie On Reggae Woman

38.	39.	40.	41.
I Am Woman	Just Like a Woman	Pretty Woman	Honky Tonk Woman

POINTS:

Beatlemania!
YEAH! YEAH! YEAH!

44.

The Beatles performed or lent their names to four films, one TV special, and one cartoon series. Name them.

42.

Who is the youngest Beatle?

43.

Who is the shortest Beatle?

45.
Paul McCartney and Wings wrote and sang the title song to what James Bond film?

46.
McCartney also wrote a hit song for the 1971 film *The Magic Christian* starring Peter Sellers and Ringo Starr. What was the name of the song?

47.
Who sang the above song?

48.
For a long time, John Lennon was the only married Beatle. What was his first wife's name?

49.
Who is John's current wife?

50.
Which of the Beatles was the Walrus?

51.
Who was Paul's long-time actress flame?

52.
What two Beatle songs released since 1965 don't appear on any of their albums?

P O I N T S :

53. True or false? *Abbey Road* was recorded before *Let It Be*.

_____

_____

54. True or false? The psychedelic single "Strawberry Fields Forever" was released before the *Sgt. Pepper's Lonely Hearts Club Band* album.

_____

_____

55. What was the first Beatles album released on Apple Records?

_____

_____

56. What was the first number-one song the Beatles had in the USA?

_____

_____

57. What was their last hit single as a group?

_____

_____

58. What was the name of the album on which John and Yoko were nude on the cover?

_____

_____

59. In the summer of 1969, a Beatles single was banned from AM radio play in many towns (including New York) for being sacrilegious, yet still made it to number nine on the charts. What was the name of the song?

_____

60. The Beatles' albums often had very "distinctive" titles. Which title does not belong to a Beatles album: a. The Beatles b. Meet the Beatles c. Introducing the Beatles d. The Early Beatles e. The Beatles Second Album f. Beatles '65 g. Beatles VI h. The Beatles 1962–1967 i. The Beatles Captured Live at the Felt Forum

_____

61. Who was the Beatles' manager?

_____

62. Who produced all of the Beatles' albums except *Let It Be?*

_____

_____

63. Ringo was a late addition to the Beatles. Whom did he replace?

_____

_____

64. What George Harrison tune did a judge say was too close to "He's So Fine" by the Chiffons?

_____

_____

65. Who was the Beatles' spiritual Indian guru?

_____

_____

66. What was the title of McCartney's first single after the group split? a. Maybe I'm Amazed b. Maybe I'm a Man c. Maybe I'm Really Dead d. Maybe e. Maybelline

_____

_____

67. Name Ringo's first six albums since the split.

_____

_____

68. Ringo starred in a Frank Zappa movie as the world's largest dwarf. What was the name of that memorable movie?

_____

_____

69. Who hasn't John Lennon recorded with since the Beatles broke up? a. Ringo Starr b. Yoko Ono c. The Plastic Ono Band d. Elephant's Memory e. Elton John f. Lawrence Welk and the Champagne Musicmakers

_____

_____

70. Which Beatles single was the longest they ever recorded?

_____

_____

71. Which mid-60's word did not describe the Beatles: a. Fab b. Gear c. Mod d. Psychedelic e. Carbonated

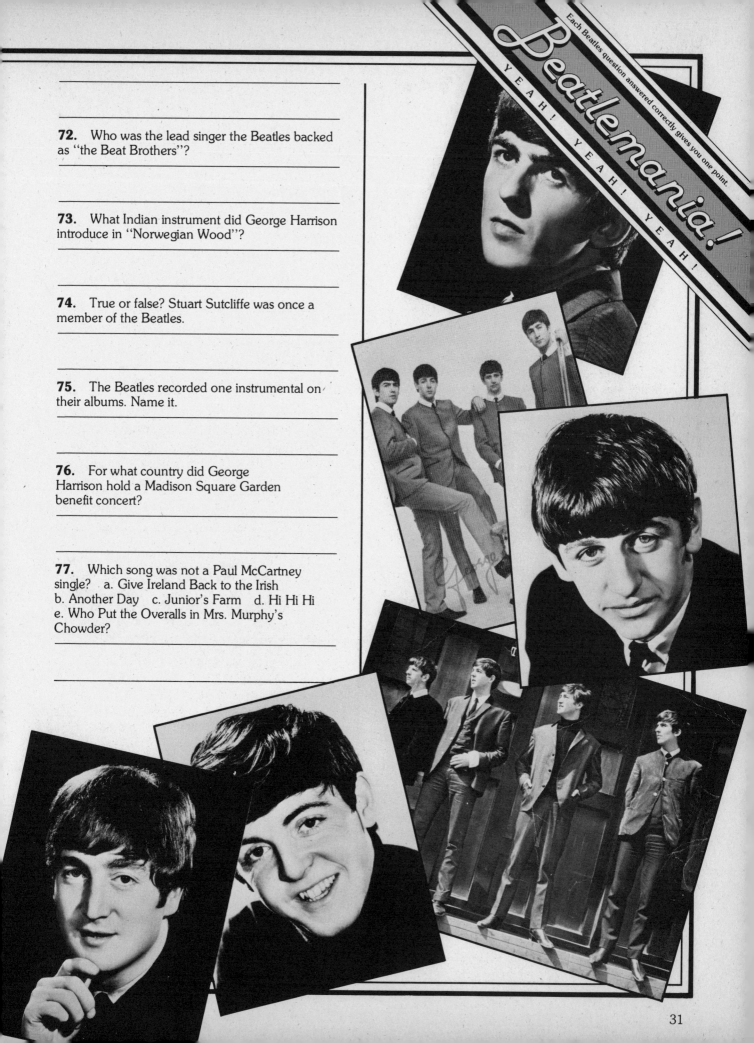

72. Who was the lead singer the Beatles backed as "the Beat Brothers"?

73. What Indian instrument did George Harrison introduce in "Norwegian Wood"?

74. True or false? Stuart Sutcliffe was once a member of the Beatles.

75. The Beatles recorded one instrumental on their albums. Name it.

76. For what country did George Harrison hold a Madison Square Garden benefit concert?

77. Which song was not a Paul McCartney single?   a. Give Ireland Back to the Irish   b. Another Day   c. Junior's Farm   d. Hi Hi Hi   e. Who Put the Overalls in Mrs. Murphy's Chowder?

BEATLES
STANDING THERE
OLD YOUR HAND

Capitol RECORDS 5112

78. In 1969, Paul McCartney was "dead." Name as many clues as you can remember from these songs or albums: a. "Revolution No. 9" b. *Abbey Road* c. *Sgt. Pepper* d. *Magical Mystery Tour* e. "Strawberry Fields Forever"

79. On what show did the Beatles make their first American TV appearance?

80. On what TV show did they perform "Hey Jude" and "Revolution"?

81. True or false? The Beatles appeared on both *Shindig* and *Hullabaloo*.

82. In the early days, the Beatles recorded some songs first done by other artists. Which singer did they re-record? a. Chuck Berry b. Little Richard c. Carl Perkins d. The Isley Brothers e. The Miracles f. Larry Williams g. The Cookies h. The Shirelles i. The Marvelettes j. All of the above

83. What were the only two Beatles songs written by Ringo alone?

84. What were the first two old Beatles' songs to be released as singles in 1976, years after the group had broken up?

85. The white album contained a song called "Martha My Dear." Who was Martha?

86. Where in New York did the Beatles perform live?

87. What was unusual about the jackets popularized by the Beatles in 1964–65?

88. Judging from the lyrics of the song, where did someone tell the Beatles to stick "Penny Lane"?

89. Which of the following were not 45-rpm records of the Beatles: a. She Loves You, All My Loving, I Want to Hold Your Hand b. Do You Want to Know a Secret, Twist and Shout, Love Me Do c. Because, Glad All Over, Bits and Pieces d. P.S. I Love You, There's a Place, Please Please Me, This Boy e. I Saw Her Standing There, Paperback Writer, Lady Madonna, Nowhere Man

T O T A L   P O I N T S :

The Leader the of Pack!

Name the groups that these performers led for one point each.

94.	95.	96.	97.
Little Anthony	Little Caesar	Joey Dee	Archie Bell
102.	**103.**	**104.**	**105.**
Huey "Piano" Smith	Eric Burdon	Cliff Richards	Bill Haley
110.	**111.**	**112.**	**113.**
Mitch Ryder	Lee Andrews	Booker T.	Arlene Smith
118.	**119.**	**120.**	**121.**
James Brown	B. Bumble	Gladys Knight	Sonny Til
126.	**127.**	**128.**	**129.**
Patty Lace	Billy J. Kramer	Spanky MacFarland	Sylvester Stewa

90.	91.	92.	93.
Buddy Holly	Martha Reeves	Bob B. Soxx	Gary Lewis

98.	99.	100.	101.
Maurice Williams	Tommy James	Duane Eddy	Junior Walker

106.	107.	108.	109.
Sam the Sham	Kathy Young	Frankie Lymon	Linda Ronstadt

114.	115.	116.	117.
Gary Puckett	Hank Ballard	Dickie Do	Wayne Fontana

122.	123.	124.	125.
John Fred	Paul Revere	Desmond Dekker	Patti LaBelle

130.	131.	132.	Points:
Max Frost	Bo Donaldson	Kenny Rogers	

Number Please!

133. _____ Dog Night

134. _____ Estate

135. Dave Clark _____

136. _____ Satins

137. Brasil _____ or _____

138. The Classics _____

139. Unit _____ Plus _____

140. MC _____

141. _____ Freshmen

142. _____ Preps

143. _____ Lads

144. We _____

145. _____ Edition

146. Brothers _____

147. _____ Dimension

148. _____ Degrees

149. _____ Aces

150. Jive _____

151. Pastel _____

152. _____ Tops

153. Jackson _____

154. Fantastic _____

155. _____ Stairsteps

156. _____ Seasons

157. _____ Years After

158. Bobby Fuller _____

159. The Ivy _____

160. Kirby Stone _____

161. _____ Wheel Drive

162. _____ Discs Group

Points: _____

As we were growing up, rumors often spread through school that some rock 'n' roll songs actually had obscene or dirty lyrics. The following is a list of actual 45-rpm records. Which of them were supposedly dirty? Write yes or no after each one for one point.

Dirty

163. The Happy Organ

164. Easy to Be Hard

165. Eli's Coming

166. Louie, Louie

167. Lay Lady Lay

168. Red Rubber Ball

169. Stay Awhile

170. Raunchy

171. She Blew a Good Thing

172. What in the World's Come Over You

173. Peppermint Stick

174. I Rise, I Fall

175. Killer Joe

176. Great Balls of Fire

177. Rubber Duckie

Songs!

YES!	NO!

TOTAL POINTS:

Award yourself one point for each question about the Monkees you answer correctly.

MONKEE BUSINESS!

178. What was the Monkees' first hit single?

179. Which Monkee had starred in the TV series *Circus Boy* when he was a child?

180. Which Monkee starred in the Broadway production of *Oliver?*

181. Which of the following was the name of the Monkees' motion picture: a. Monkee Business   b. Monkee on My Back   c. Monkees'   d. Head

182. Which Monkee was the only one capable of playing a musical instrument when their television show started?

183. Which Monkee was the first to quit the group?

184. What was Mike's nickname?

185. What instrument did Mickey play on the show?

186. The Monkees were the first group to record on a new record label. What was the name of the label?

187. The Monkees have re-formed, with some new members replacing some old ones. Name the four new Monkees.

Points: _____

BRYLCREEM® PRESENTS
SING ALONG WITH
CONNIE FRANCIS
an MGM recording artist

Encore Of Golden Hits
THE PLATTERS
THE GREAT PRETENDER   MY PRAYER
TWILIGHT TIME   ONLY YOU
SMOKE GETS IN YOUR EYES   REMEMBER WHEN
THE MAGIC TOUCH   MY DREAM
ENCHANTED   HEAVEN ON EARTH
ONE IN A MILLION   I'M SORRY

Mercury
RECORDS
HIGH FIDELITY
Custom

Food Glor

Food has always been an integral part of rock 'n' roll. You don't believe it? Well just take a look at this list of songs with different foods in the titles and name the groups that ate or sang them. Each is worth one point.

POINTS:

ous Food!!

Yummy, Yummy, Chewy, Chewy, FOOIE, FOOIE!

How well do you know bubble-gum music? Each question is worth 1 point except the ID's. Give yourself 5 points if you answer them correctly after Clue A, 3 points after Clue B, or 1 point after Clue C.

213.

A.	I was a prepubescent girls' heartthrob in the late 60's to early 70's.
B.	I co-starred in the TV show *Here Come the Brides*.
C.	I recorded hits like "Easy Come, Easy Go" for Metromedia Records.
My name is?	**Points:**

214.

A.	I, too, was a prepubescent girls' heartthrob in the early 70's.
B.	I co-starred in the TV show *The Partridge Family*.
C.	I recorded hits like "I Woke Up in Love This Morning" for Bell Records.
My name is?	**Points:**

215.

A.	I am a singer from Montreal who once sang with the Archies.
B.	My first big hit was a bubble-gum remake of "Baby, I Love You."
C.	I made a comeback in 1974 with "Rock Me Gently."
My name is?	**Points:**

216. According to "Yummy, Yummy, Yummy," what have I got in my tummy?

218. Who was the musical mastermind behind the Archies?

217. The Archies were a studio group put together for a cartoon show. On "Sugar, Sugar," who was the lead singer?

219. What group had hit singles with kids' games such as "Simon Says" and "One, Two, Three Red Light"?

220.

Which of these tunes about a candy girl got The Archies wanting her?

a. Candy Girl

b. Candy Man

c. My Boy Lollipop

d. Sugar, Sugar

e. Garbage, Garbage

221.

In which song did Bobby Sherman tell his baby to remember—he'll be back September?

a. See You in September

b. Sealed with a Kiss

c. Bang Shang-a-Lang

d. Julie, Do You Love Me?

e. Summertime, Summertime

222.

Which group sang "Quick Joey Small"?

a. The Ohio Express

b. The Lemon Pipers

c. The 1910 Fruitgum Company

d. The Grassroots

e. The Katznitz-Katz Singing Orchestral Circus

223.

The Ohio Express had recording success with which of these songs?

a. Does Your Chewing Gum Lose Its Flavor on the Bedpost Overnight?

b. Tie Me Kangaroo Down

c. Chewy, Chewy

d. Santa Claus Is Watching You

e. Inna Gadda Da Vida

Total Points:

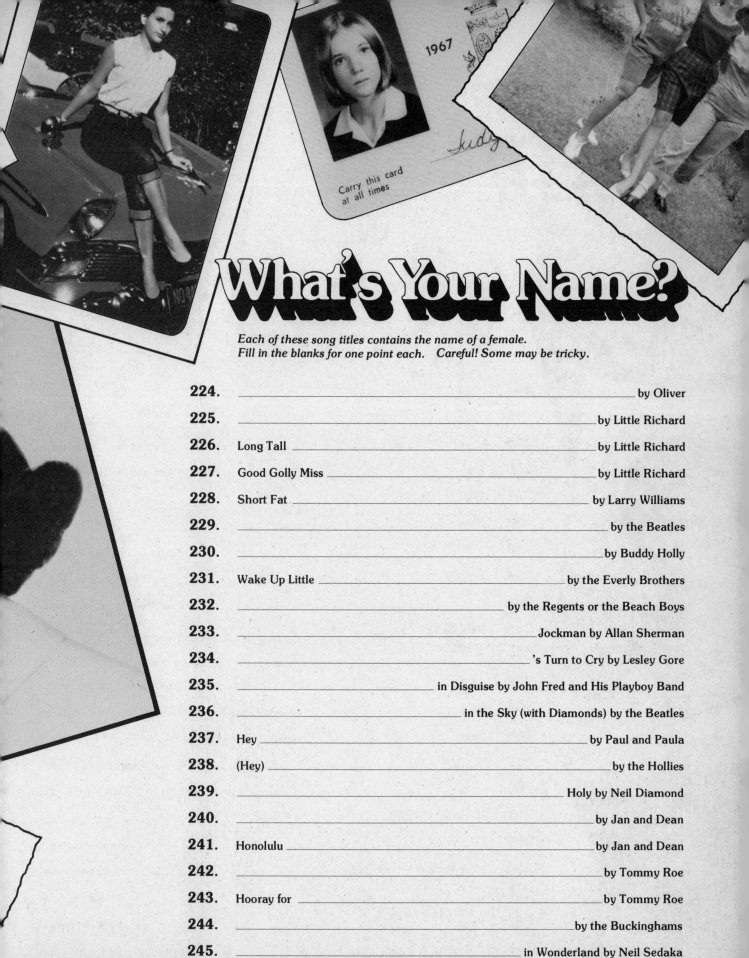

Carry this card
at all times

What's Your Name?

Each of these song titles contains the name of a female.
Fill in the blanks for one point each.   Careful! Some may be tricky.

224. _____ by Oliver

225. _____ by Little Richard

226. Long Tall _____ by Little Richard

227. Good Golly Miss _____ by Little Richard

228. Short Fat _____ by Larry Williams

229. _____ by the Beatles

230. _____ by Buddy Holly

231. Wake Up Little _____ by the Everly Brothers

232. _____ by the Regents or the Beach Boys

233. _____ Jockman by Allan Sherman

234. _____ 's Turn to Cry by Lesley Gore

235. _____ in Disguise by John Fred and His Playboy Band

236. _____ in the Sky (with Diamonds) by the Beatles

237. Hey _____ by Paul and Paula

238. (Hey) _____ by the Hollies

239. _____ Holy by Neil Diamond

240. _____ by Jan and Dean

241. Honolulu _____ by Jan and Dean

242. _____ by Tommy Roe

243. Hooray for _____ by Tommy Roe

244. _____ by the Buckinghams

245. _____ in Wonderland by Neil Sedaka

246. _____ by the Four Seasons

45

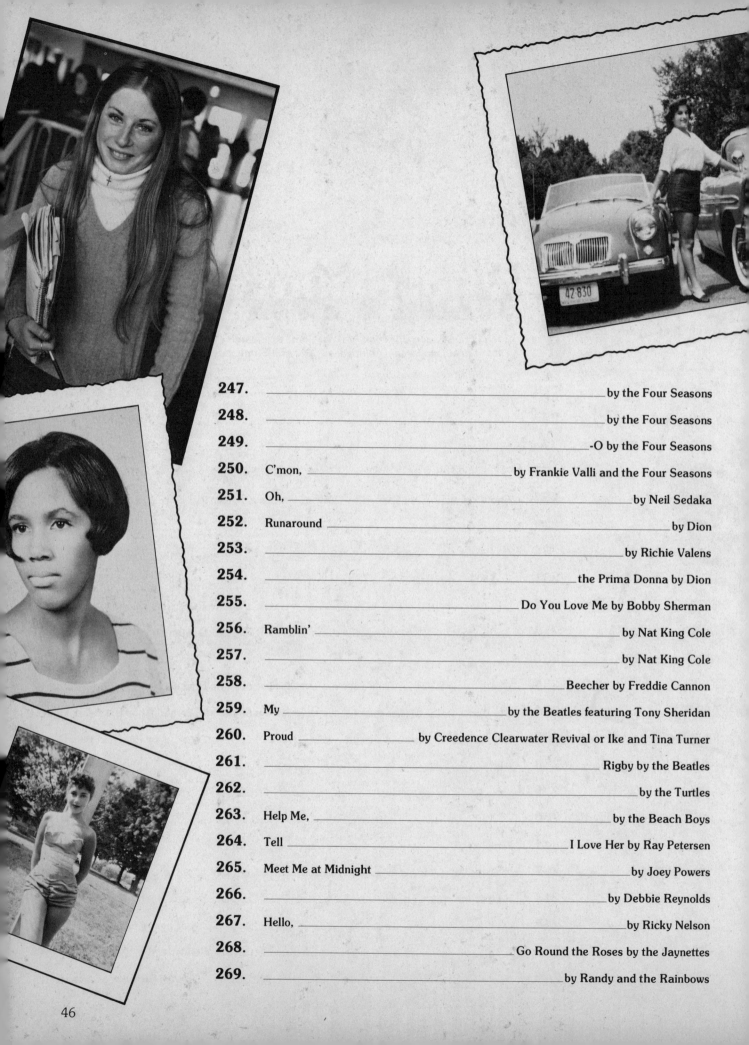

247. _____ by the Four Seasons

248. _____ by the Four Seasons

249. _____ -O by the Four Seasons

250. C'mon, _____ by Frankie Valli and the Four Seasons

251. Oh, _____ by Neil Sedaka

252. Runaround _____ by Dion

253. _____ by Richie Valens

254. _____ the Prima Donna by Dion

255. _____ Do You Love Me by Bobby Sherman

256. Ramblin' _____ by Nat King Cole

257. _____ by Nat King Cole

258. _____ Beecher by Freddie Cannon

259. My _____ by the Beatles featuring Tony Sheridan

260. Proud _____ by Creedence Clearwater Revival or Ike and Tina Turner

261. _____ Rigby by the Beatles

262. _____ by the Turtles

263. Help Me, _____ by the Beach Boys

264. Tell _____ I Love Her by Ray Petersen

265. Meet Me at Midnight _____ by Joey Powers

266. _____ by Debbie Reynolds

267. Hello, _____ by Ricky Nelson

268. _____ Go Round the Roses by the Jaynettes

269. _____ by Randy and the Rainbows

46

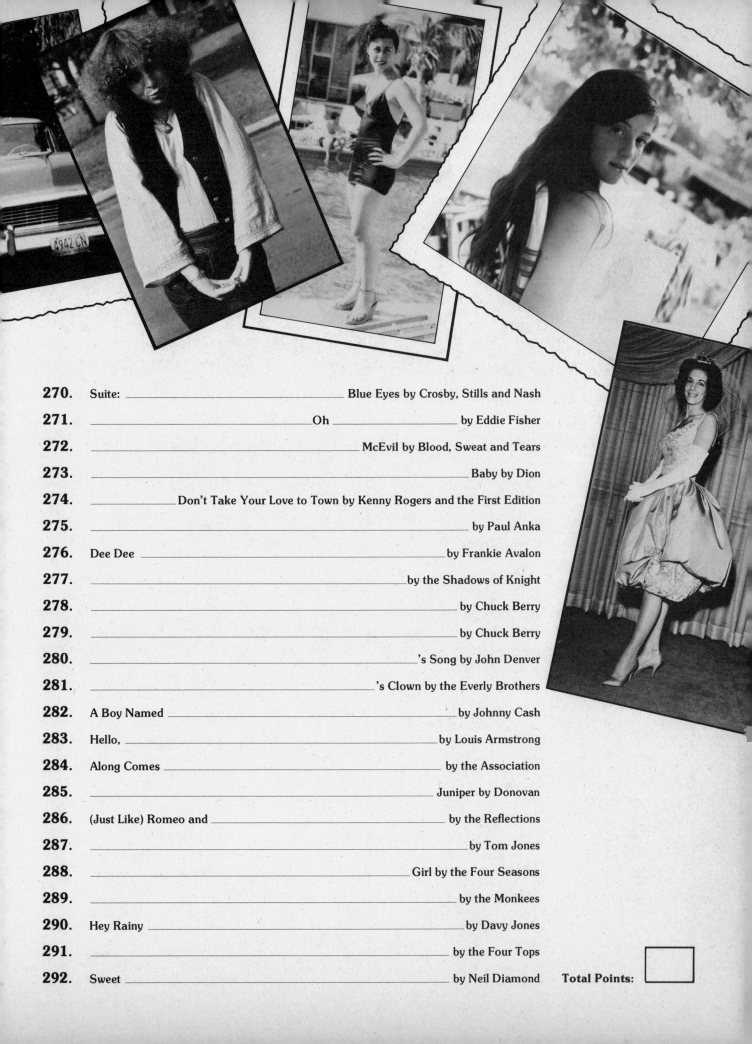

270. Suite: _____ Blue Eyes by Crosby, Stills and Nash

271. _____ Oh _____ by Eddie Fisher

272. _____ McEvil by Blood, Sweat and Tears

273. _____ Baby by Dion

274. _____ Don't Take Your Love to Town by Kenny Rogers and the First Edition

275. _____ by Paul Anka

276. Dee Dee _____ by Frankie Avalon

277. _____ by the Shadows of Knight

278. _____ by Chuck Berry

279. _____ by Chuck Berry

280. _____ 's Song by John Denver

281. _____ 's Clown by the Everly Brothers

282. A Boy Named _____ by Johnny Cash

283. Hello, _____ by Louis Armstrong

284. Along Comes _____ by the Association

285. _____ Juniper by Donovan

286. (Just Like) Romeo and _____ by the Reflections

287. _____ by Tom Jones

288. _____ Girl by the Four Seasons

289. _____ by the Monkees

290. Hey Rainy _____ by Davy Jones

291. _____ by the Four Tops

292. Sweet _____ by Neil Diamond   Total Points: ☐

MISH-

One point for each question you correctly answer about this and that.

293. Which of the following "brothers" groups never had a hit record: a. Allman Brothers b. Mills Brothers c. Righteous Brothers d. Brothers Four e. Smith Brothers f. Everly Brothers g. Cornelius Brothers and Sister Rose h. Isley Brothers i. Chambers Brothers

294. Which is the correct statement: a. There was a hit song called "Silhouettes" by the Rays. b. There was a hit song called "Rays" by the Silhouettes. c. Both of the above are true.

295. Which of the following rock 'n' roll groups named after cars did *not* exist: a. The Fleetwoods b. The El Dorados c. The Cadillacs d. The Edsels e. The Mustangs f. The Packards g. The Impalas h. The Rivieras i. The Imperials j. The Capris

296. Which of the following songs had nothing to do with cars: a. Cara Mia b. GTO c. 409 d. Hot Rod Lincoln e. Beep Beep f. Little Deuce Coupe g. Dead Man's Curve h. Little Honda i. Tell Laura I Love Her

297. Which of the following songs is *not* a real "moon" song: a. Blue Moon b. There's a Moon Out Tonight c. Mr. Moonlight d. Moon River e. Allegheny Moon f. There's a Moon Hanging Out of Your Car Window Tonight

298. Match the artist to the record label:

Stevie Wonder	Mercury
Chuck Berry	Specialty
Little Richard	Parkway
The Platters	Tamla
Chubby Checker	Chess

299. Before they became the group Labelle, they were merely Patty LaBelle and the Blue-Belles. Which of these songs was the earlier group's greatest hit: a. I Sold My Heart to the Junkman b. I Sold My Body to the Milkman c. I Sold My Raisins to the Raisin Man d. I Sold My Organs to the Smithsonian e. I Sold My Nuts to the Peanut Man

300. It's possible that Sammy Davis, Jr., was suffering from an inferiority complex when he asked the musical question: a. What Kind of Dope Am I? b. What Kind of Jerk Am I? c. What Kind of Moron Am I? d. What Kind of Fool Am I? e. What Kind of Nerd Am I?

301. Cities have soared to fame in song, but which pair of songs actually immortalized the Queen City of Cincinnati: a. My Boyfriend's Name Is Fatty Who Comes From Cincinnati and Cincinnati Ain't So Ratty b. Batty Over Cincinnati and The Monster that Stomped Cincinnati c. The Cincinnati Dancing Pig and The Cockroach That Ate Cincinnati d. The Last Train from Cincy and The Eggplant That Threw Up on Cincinnati e. Hello to Morrie and Anne Osher in Cincinnati and Syd Litvack Smokes Cincinnati Stogies

302. True or false? David Seville of David Seville and the Chipmunks is a real person.

303. Which of these real "fine" songs was *not* a 45-rpm record: a. A Love So Fine b. Another Fine Mess c. He's So Fine d. One Fine Day e. So Fine f. Feel So Fine

304. Match the "happy" song to the artist who recorded it:

Oh Happy Day	Jimmy Soul
Oh How Happy	Dave "Baby" Cortez
Happy Days	The Tuneweavers
Happy Birthday Sweet 16	Neil Sedaka
Happy, Happy Birthday Baby	Shades of Blue
The Happy Organ	The Edwin Hawkins Singers
If You Wanna Be Happy	Pratt and McClain
Happy Together	The Turtles

305. KEEPING UP WITH THE JONESES. Which of the following was Joe Jones' hit single: a. You Talk Too Much b. You Eat Too Much c. You Sleep Too Much d. You Runaround Too Much e. You Belch Too Much

306. KEEPING UP WITH THE JONESES, PART II. Which of the following was Tom Jones' hit single: a. It's Not Uncommon b. It's Not Useful c. It's Not Unusual d. It's Not Usual e. It's Not Useless

307. KEEPING UP WITH THE JONESES, PART III. Which of the following was Jack Jones' hit single: a. Call Me Irresponsible b. Call Me Unscrupulous c. Call Me Inadequate d. Call Me Impotent e. Call Me a Cab

308. KEEPING UP WITH THE JONESES, PART IV. Which of the following was Jimmy Jones' hit single: a. Candy Man b. Handy Man c. Sandy Man d. Dandy Man e. Randy Man

Points:

FROM THE MOTION PICTURE

Rock, Rock

THE MOONGLOWS
CHUCK • BERRY
THE FLAMINGOS

THE EVERLY BROTHERS

50

51

309. Elvis Presley's personal manager for years was:
a. Colonel Sanders   b. Captain Binghamton
c. Colonel Parker   d. Ensign Parker
e. General Mills

_____

_____

310. On his first major television appearance, Elvis was photographed from the waist up because his gyrations were considered too obscene by the network. What show did Elvis appear on?
a. *Hollywood Palace*   b. *The Ed Sullivan Show*
c. *Broadway Open House*   d. *The Tonight Show*
e. *Sermonette*

_____

_____

311. In the song "All Shook Up," what was Elvis itching like?

_____

_____

312. Which of the following songs was not originally popularized by Elvis: a. Whole Lotta Shakin' Goin' On   b. Are You Lonesome Tonight?   c. Can't Help Falling in Love   d. Hard Headed Woman   e. Teddy Bear

_____

313. In "Hound Dog," why won't you ever be a friend of Elvis'?

_____

_____

314. What famous song was on the flip-side of "Hound Dog"?

_____

_____

315. What was the name of Elvis' back-up group:
a. The Preslettes   b. Sons of the Pioneers   c. The Hound Dogs   d. The Jordanaires   e. The All Night Newsboys

_____

316. What is the name of the street on which you'll find Heartbreak Hotel?

_____

_____

317. In what song did Elvis make the philosophic statement that tomorrow would be today?

_____

_____

318. What was the name of Elvis' first motion picture: a. *Kid Gallahad*   b. *Viva Las Vegas*
c. *Roustabout*   d. *Love Me Tender*   e. *It's Now or Never*

_____

319. What did Elvis name his estate in Nashville?
a. Gracie Mansion   b. George and Gracie's Place
c. Graceland   d. Roseland   e. The Hound Dog Spa

_____

320. Fill in the blanks to these Elvis hit songs:
a. In the _____
b. I _____ You, I _____ You, I _____ You
c. _____ in Disguise
d. Crying in the _____
e. _____ Rock

Points: _____

ON
RCA VICTOR
47-8100
45 RPM
ELVIS
SINGS
RETURN TO
SENDER
and
WHERE DO YOU
COME FROM
From the Paramount Picture
GIRLS, GIRLS, GIRLS
A HAL WALLIS PRODU

Ask your dealer about ELVIS

52

Elvis Pelvis!

Each question you answer correctly about the King of Rock 'n' Roll is worth one point.

All of the following song titles contain the word "Mr.," "Mrs.," or "Miss." Give yourself one point for each blank correctly filled in.

Mr., Mrs. and Miss!

Total Points:

321.	_____ Blue
322.	_____ Robinson
323.	Good Golly _____ Molly
324.	_____ Custer
325.	_____ Moonlight
326.	Please _____ Postman
327.	_____ Brown, You've Got a Lovely Daughter
328.	_____ Sandman
329.	_____ Tambourine Man
330.	Theme from _____ Lucky
331.	Me and _____ Jones
332.	_____ Lee
333.	I Shot _____ Lee
334.	Walkin' with _____ Lee
335.	I'm the Jivin' _____ Lee
336.	_____ Bass Man
337.	_____ Bojangles
338.	_____ D.J.
339.	_____ Lonely
340.	_____ Bongos

Name the groups that rocketed these dances to fame for one point each.

Do You Wanna Dance?   POINTS: _____

(Baby) Hully Gully	The Peppermint Twist	The Fly	Pony Time
345.	346.	347.	348.
The Mouse	Blame It on the Bossa Nova	Monkey Time	The Locomotion
353.	354.	355.	356.

54

Clothes Call!

361. *Match the musical apparel to the well-dressed singer for one point each!* **Points:**

A White Sport Coat and a Pink Carnation	The Drifters
Tan Shoes with Pink Shoe Laces	The Big Bopper
Blue Suede Shoes	The Royal Teens
Bobbie Socks to Stockings	Dodie Stevens
Venus in Blue Jeans	Brian Hyland
Black Denim Trousers	Carl Perkins
These Boots Are Made for Walking	Connie Francis
Chantilly Lace	Frankie Avalon
Lipstick on Your Collar	The Cheers
Penny Loafers and Bobby Sox	Marty Robbins
Sand in My Shoes	Nancy Sinatra
Short Shorts	Jimmy Clanton
Itsy Bitsy Teeny Weeny Yellow Polka Dot Bikini	Joe Bennett and the Sparkletones

Cool Jerk	Wah-Watusi	The Bristol Stomp	The Swim
341.	*342.*	*343.*	*344.*
The Limbo Rock	**Mashed Potato Time**	**The Stroll**	**The Freddie**
349.	*350.*	*351.*	*352.*
The Jerk	**The Watusi**	**The Hucklebuck**	**The Hustle**
357.	*358.*	*359.*	*360.*

Give yourself one point for each Motown question you can answer.

362. Where is Motown Records now headquartered?

_____

363. True or false? Between 1964 and 1974, Marvin Gaye was the male singer with the most songs in the Top Ten.

_____

364. What was Marvin Gaye's first number-one single?

_____

_____

365. One of Motown's favorite ploys was to team up Marvin Gaye with a female singer to crank out hit records. Which singer did Marvin *not* sing a duet with: a. Tammi Terrell   b. Mary Wells   c. Kim Weston   d. Diana Ross   e. Dinah Shore

_____

_____

366. True or false? Motown had a hit with "Ain't That Gay?" by Marvin Peculiar.

_____

367. What was Stevie Wonder's first hit record?

_____

_____

368. Now Stevie Wonder is well known for playing the synthesizer. What instrument did he first become famous with?

_____

_____

369. How old was Stevie Wonder when he made his first hit record?

_____

370. Who had hits with "Jimmy Mack," "Quicksand," and "Heatwave"?

_____

371. Who had hits with "Too Many Fish in the Sea," "My Baby Must Be a Magician," and "Please, Mr. Postman"?

372. Who had hits with "Just My Imagination," "Beauty's Only Skin Deep," and "Ain't Too Proud to Beg"?

_____

373. Who had hits with "Signed, Sealed, Delivered I'm Yours," "I Was Made to Love Her," and "Uptight"?

_____

374. Who had hits with "You Beat Me to the Punch," "Two Lovers," and "My Guy"?

_____

For these next two ID questions, give yourself 5 points if you can name the person after Clue A, 3 points after Clue B, and 1 point after Clue C.

375. A. I am a vice president with Motown. B. I am the poet laureate of Motown, having penned many hits. C. I sang for years with the Miracles before going solo. I am?

_____

376. A. We are from Gary, Indiana. B. We were discovered by Diana Ross. C. We had a TV cartoon series to go along with hits like "ABC" and "Dancin' Machine." We are?

377. Which of these record labels is *not* owned by Motown: a. Tamla b. Gordy c. MoWest d. MoMoney e. Soul

378. Who recorded an album entitled *Evets Rednow*?

379. Motown's first big hit was "Shop Around." Who recorded it?

380. Another early Motown hit was "Money"— later recorded by the Beatles. Who did the original for Motown?

381. Who had hits with "First I Look at the Purse," "Shake Sherry," and "Do You Love Me"?

Points:

The Grateful Dead!

Most rock songs have to do with love. Then there are a lot of records that sing about cars. But next on the teen hit parade were songs about death. For a while in the early sixties, Top Forty radio sounded like one long ad for funeral parlors. Rock 'n' Roll heroes and heroines met untimely ends in car crashes, train wrecks, and gunfights. We pause for a moment of silent tribute to honor those who lived and died on seven-inch discs of polyvinyl chloride and are now in that great rock 'n' roll heaven.

Identify the song and the artist for one point each (or a possible two points for each question).

382. It happened on a fateful night when a car stalled on a railroad track.

383. He looked and saw his sweater lying on her grave.

384. He was pulled from a twisted wreck, and with his dying breath he said . . .

385. He can't find his baby anywhere, because the Lord took her away from him.

386. As he left her on that rainy night, she begged him to go slow.

387. His folks were always putting his girlfriend down because her laundry came back brown.

388. His girl wrecked the car and was so afraid that he'd be mad. But he thought what the heck.

389. The last thing he remembered, he told his doctor, was starting to swerve, when he saw the Jag slide into the curve.

P O I N T S :

HOMETOWN HONEYS!

390. *Match the singer or group with their hometown for one point each.*

Dion and the Belmonts	Portland, Oregon
Gerry and the Pacemakers	Sweden
Jefferson Airplane	Jersey City, New Jersey
Bobby Rydell	Los Angeles, California
The Buckinghams	Toronto, Canada
KC and the Sunshine Band	Liverpool, England
Paul Anka	Boston, Massachusetts
The Rolling Stones	St. Louis, Missouri
The Doors	Memphis, Tennessee
Kool and the Gang	Bronx, New York
Little Richard	Kingston, Jamaica
Abba	San Francisco, California
The Kingsmen	Hibbings, Minnesota
The Supremes	Jacksonville, Florida
Bob Dylan	Macon, Georgia
Helen Reddy	London, England
Chuck Berry	Chicago, Illinois
Bob Marley and the Wailers	Philadelphia, Pennsylvania
Orpheus	Detroit, Michigan
Elvis Presley	Australia

Points: _____

The Great American Novelty Song!

Many songs had sequels or parodies recorded as a musical response to the hits. What were the actual hits that these novelty songs were based on? Give yourself one point for every correct answer!

391. **Leader of the Laundromat** _____

392. **Son-in-Law** _____

393. **Oh, Neil** _____

394. **Duchess of Earl** _____

395. **Small Sad Sam** _____

396. **Mrs. Schwartz, You've Got an Ugly Daughter** _____

397. **Queen of the House** _____

398. **Battle of Kookamonga** _____

399. **A Girl Named Johnny Cash** _____

POINTS: _____

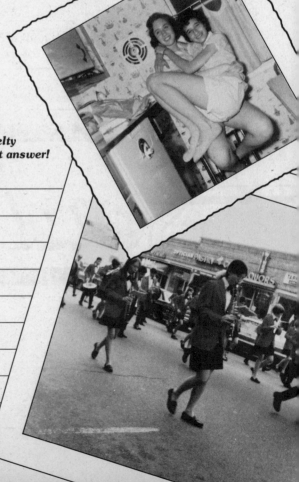

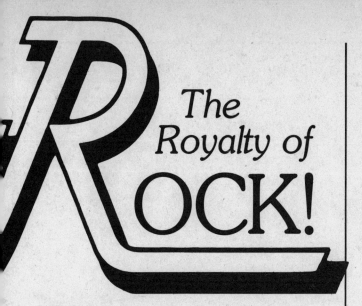

The Royalty of ROCK!

The following singers and groups have titles of royalty in their names. With all the proper etiquette at your command, fill in the blanks with the proper title for one point. Then get ready to play the Palace!

400. B. B. _____

401. The Teen _____ s

402. Carole _____

403. The Amboy _____ s

404. Nat _____ Cole

405. _____ Curtis and the _____ pins

406. The _____ Douglas Quintet

407. The _____ smen

408. Ben E. _____

409. The Mello- _____ s

P O I N T S :

410. Sh-Boom _____

411. Oom Dooby Doom _____

412. Zip A Dee Doo Dah _____

413. Sha La La _____

414. Shimmy Shimmy Ko Ko Bop _____

415. Um Um Um Um Um Um _____

416. Nah Nah Hey Hey Kiss Him Goodbye _____

417. Nee Nee Na Na Na Na Nu Nu _____

418. Beep Beep _____

419. Rama Lama Ding Dong _____

420. My Ding A Ling _____

421. Da Doo Ron Ron _____

422. Alley Oop _____

423. La La Means I Love You _____

424. Ya-Ya _____

425. Bang Shang A Lang _____

426. Mamma Look A Boo Boo _____

427. Papa Oom Mow Mow _____

428. Ob La Di Ob La Da _____

429. Doo Wah Diddy _____

430. Chick A Boom _____

431. Loop De Loop _____

432. Tweedlee Dee _____

CRAZY TITLES!

Name the artists who sang these typical 1950's style songs with crazy words in the title. Each is worth 2 points.

POINTS: _____

59

T

FOR TWO

433. Match the singer or group to the "T" song for 2 points each. This quiz really isn't any more difficult than those worth only 1 point apiece, but how could we name a quiz "T for One"?

a.	Tower of Strength	The Chambers Brothers
b.	Tossin' and Turnin'	The Classics IV
c.	Tell Him	The Crests
d.	Take Good Care of My Baby	Johnny Rivers
e.	Trouble in Paradise	Three Dog Night
f.	This Will Be	Bobby Lewis
g.	Tonite, Tonite	The Byrds
h.	Turn Me Loose	Lou Christie
i.	Turn! Turn! Turn!	Little Anthony and the Imperials
j.	Turn Down Day	Bobby Vee
k.	Traces	Bachman–Turner Overdrive
l.	Time of the Season	The Exciters
m.	Time Has Come Today	The Fleetwoods
n.	Tears on My Pillow	Natalie Cole
o.	Tracks of My Tears	The Cyrkle
p.	Tragedy	Gene McDaniels
q.	To the Aisle	The Zombies
r.	Try a Little Tenderness	The Mello-Kings
s.	Two Faces Have I	The Five Satins
t.	Taking Care of Business	Fabian
Points:		

Dynamic Duos!

434. For one point each, fill in the missing partner.

			A.
			Chad and

B.	C.	D.	E.
Peter and	Ian and	Mickey and	Shirley and

F.	G.	H.	I.
Billy and	Simon and	Jan and	Sam and

J.	K.	L.	M.
Don and	Johnnie and	Nino Tempo and	Dick and

N.	O.	P.	Points:
Paul and	Sonny and	Seals and	

The Supreme Sacrifice!

Diana Ross, Mary Wilson, and the late Florence Ballard made up the biggest female singing group of the mid-60's. Give yourself one point for every correct answer about the resplendently coiffured and gowned Supremes.

435. For what record label did the Supremes do their singing?

436. The Supremes were the first singing group to have six consecutive number-one records in one year. Name them.

437. Florence Ballard was the first Supreme to quit the group. Who replaced her?

438. Diana Ross eventually left the Supremes to pursue a solo career. Who replaced Diana as the Supremes' lead singer?

439. What was the last hit single the Supremes had with Diana Ross?

440. What was the first hit the Supremes had without Diana Ross?

441. Who were the songwriters responsible for Diana Ross and the Supremes early hits?

442. The Supremes had a hit with the title song of a 1967 movie starring Anthony Quinn. What was the song?

443. The Supremes teamed up with the Temptations to do a television special called *T.C.B.* What hit single resulted from that team-up?

444. Name three movies that have starred Diana Ross.

POINTS:

Songs That Were Instrumental to Rock'n'Roll!

Tell us which of these songs were instrumentals. Answer yes or no for one point each.

Points: ☐

445.	☐	Sleep Walk
446.	☐	Walkin' My Baby Back Home
447.	☐	Walk Don't Run
448.	☐	Runaway
449.	☐	Love Is Blue
450.	☐	Love Is Strange
451.	☐	Stranger on the Shore
452.	☐	Rinky Dink
453.	☐	Honky Tonk
454.	☐	Windy
455.	☐	Cast Your Fate to the Wind
456.	☐	Exodus
457.	☐	Go Away, Little Girl
458.	☐	Pipeline
459.	☐	Wipe Out
460.	☐	Teen Beat
461.	☐	You Can't Do That
462.	☐	Scorpio
463.	☐	No Matter What Sign You Are
464.	☐	No Matter What Shape Your Stomach Is In
465.	☐	You Make Me Feel Like Dancing
466.	☐	Summer Breeze
467.	☐	Autumn Leaves
468.	☐	A Fifth of Beethoven
469.	☐	Roll Over Beethoven

In the 50's, it was Elvis Presley. In the 60's, the Beatles. And in the 70's, it's Elton John

E   L   T

470.

What is Elton John's real name?

471.

Elton first worked with a band called:
- a. Rockology
- b. Parapsychology
- c. Bluesology
- d. Hysterectomy
- e. The Elton John Band

472.

The budding rock star took his stage name from the real names of two musicians. Who were they?

473.

In the movie Tommy, what role did Elton play?

474.

Elton has shared the spotlight and microphone with other singers in the past. Whom did he record "Don't Go Breaking My Heart" with?

475.

With whom did Elton sing "Bad Blood"?

O N !

476.
What record company does Mr. John own?

477.
What musical instrument does Elton play?

478.
When it comes to songwriting, Elton John writes the music. Who puts the words in his mouth?

479.
How were Elton and his wordsmith first united:
a. by telephone
b. by his agent
c. by mail
d. bicarbonate
e. bisexually

P O I N T S

480. Name Elton John's first American album:
a. *Goodbye Yellow Brick Road*
b. *Captain Fantastic and the Brown Dirt Cowboy*
c. *Tumbleweed Connection*   d. *Don't Shoot Me—I'm Only the Piano Player*   e. *Elton John*

_____

_____

481. He wrote the soundtrack for a 1971 movie about two star-crossed lovers. Name that film.

_____

_____

482. Elton had a hit in 1975 with what Beatle song?

_____

_____

483. If his 1977 hit is any indication, what seems to be the hardest word in Elton's vocabulary?

_____

_____

484. Elton John is a sports enthusiast as well as a musician. He is the director of which of these sports teams?   a. Macon Whoopies Hockey Club
b. Manila Folders Baseball Club
c. London Bridges Cricket Club
d. Watford Hornets Soccer Club

_____

_____

485. Whom did Elton dedicate his record "Philadelphia Freedom" to?

_____

_____

486. Elton wrote a song about which former movie star?   a. Bela Lugosi   b. James Dean
c. Marilyn Monroe   d. Humphrey Bogart
e. Porky Pig

_____

_____

487. Is Elton John married?

_____

_____

488. Extremely myopic, Elton John has turned his need for spectacles into a real spectacle. He owns approximately how many pairs of glasses?   a. 1,000 pairs   b. 100 pairs   c. 20 pairs   d. 200 pairs

_____

_____

489. Elton John sang "goodbye" to something that was a part of a classic movie for the young and young-at-heart. What did he say "goodbye" to: a. The Good Ship Lollipop   b. The Absent-Minded Professor   c. Never-Never Land
d. The House on Pooh Corner   e. The Yellow Brick Road   f. Mary Poppins   g. Linda Lovelace's throat

_____

_____

Total Points:

Color
MY WORLD!

Each of these songs has a color in the title. Fill in the blank for one point each.

490. Silence is _____

491. _____ on _____

492. The _____ People Eater

493. _____ Shoes with _____ Shoelaces

494. _____ Suede Shoes

495. Tie a _____ Ribbon Round the Old Oak Tree

496. _____ Roses for a _____ Lady

497. That Old_____ Magic

498. A _____ Sport Coat and a _____ Carnation

499. _____ Velvet

500. Navy _____

501. _____ Sugar

502. _____ Sails in the Sunset

503. Mrs. _____, You've Got a Lovely Daughter

504. Paint It _____

505. Venus in _____ Jeans

506. _____ Denim Trousers (and Motorcycle Boots)

507. Summertime _____

508. The _____ Door

509. _____ Angel

510. _____ Monday

511. _____ Moon

512. Mr. _____

513. _____ Onions

514. Itsy Bitsy Teeny Weeny _____ Polka Dot Bikini

515. _____ Christmas

516. Ruby _____ Dress (Leave Me Alone)

517. Roses Are _____ My Love

518. Mellow _____

519. Devil With a _____ Dress

520. _____ Room

521. _____ Is _____

522. _____ Rubber Ball

523. _____ Submarine

524. _____ Haze

525. _____ and Clover

526. _____ Fields

527. _____ Finger

528. _____ Tambourine

529. Don't It Make My _____ Eyes _____

POINTS:

ONLY THE NAMES HAVE BEEN CHANGED TO PROTECT THE INNOCENT!

Many rock stars have changed their names on their way to fame, fortune, and disc jockeys who can't pronounce properly. Match the singer to his or her real name for one point each.

a.	Ringo Starr
b.	Bob Dylan
c.	Stevie Wonder
d.	Chubby Checker
e.	The Big Bopper
f.	Del Shannon
g.	Marcie Blane
h.	Little Richard
i.	Bobby Darin
j.	Herman of Herman's Hermits
k.	Bo Diddley
l.	Carole King
m.	David Seville
	Ellas McDaniels
	Ernest Evans
	Carol Klein
	Robert Waldon Cassatto
	Peter Noone
	Richard Starkey
	Ross Bagdasarian
	J. P. Richardson
	Marsha Blanc
	Steveland Morris
	Robert Zimmerman
	Charlie Westover
	Richard Penniman
530.	**Points:**

You Belong to Me

Featuring

WHY DON'T YOU BELIEVE ME

THE DUPREES

COED

LPC-905

Including: My Own True Love · You Belong to Me · Why Don't You Believe Me · September in the Rain · The Things I Love · Ginny · These Foolish Things · Take Me As I Am · and others

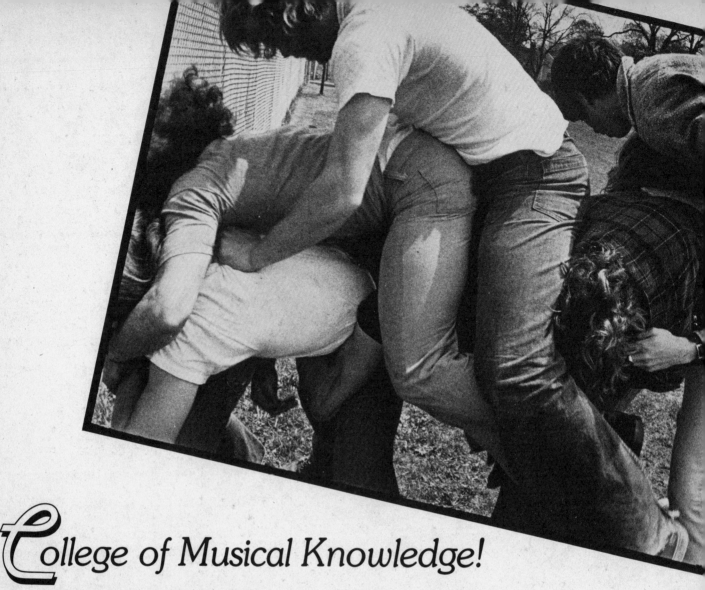

College of Musical Knowledge!

Ascend the ivory tower of rock 'n' roll scholarship with us and grade yourself 1 point for every correct answer. No extra credit for joining a sorority or going out for football.

531. He was her first and last love. She never made him blue. She was true to who?

532. Who is Sweet Loretta Martin?

533. What is the name of the happily married couple in "Ob-la-di, Ob-la-da"?

534. What group did Ringo quit to join the Beatles?

535. Where did I find my thrill?

536. What was the "handle" of the convoy leader in C. W. McCall's C.B. classic "Convoy"?

537. *I Never Felt More Like Singing the Blues Department.* Many groups have used the world "Blue" in their names. We'll give you a hit by the blue group, you give us the group's colorful name for 1 point each.   a. I'm Your Venus   b. Hooked on a Feeling   c. Bad Luck   d. Don't Fear the Reaper

538. True or false? The Band began their career as the back-up band for Ronnie Hawkins.

Family Affair!

539. Whose voices go "peep," and whose cars go "beep?" (Hint: They have no reason to live!)

_____

_____

540. In "I Get Around," why don't any of the guys go steady?

_____

_____

541. Dawn had a sister group that only had one hit record—"I Hear Those Church Bells Ringing." What is the name of Dawn's sister group?

_____

_____

542. In the song "Kansas City," what corner will I be standing on?

_____

_____

543. True or false? "Let's Make Love at the Zoo" was a big hit for the Ostriches.

_____

_____

544. Under which name did Paul Simon and Art Garfunkel record in the 1950's:
a. Herman and Catnip   b. The Kessler Twins
c. Dan Druff and the Shampoos   d. Yogi and
Boo-Boo   d. Tom and Jerry   e. Fred and Ethel
Mertz

_____

_____

POINTS:

For one point each, fill in the blanks with one of your relatives. For example, "Mother of Mercy! Is this the end of Rico?"

545. _____ Said (There'd Be Days Like This)

546. _____ 's Home

547. He Ain't Heavy, He's My _____.

548. _____ -In-Law

549. Look What They've Done To My Song, _____.

550. _____ 's Got A Brand New Bag

551. _____ Didn't Lie

552. Kissin ' _____

553. My _____

554. Down at _____Joe's

555. _____ Don't Go Near the Indians

556. My _____ Is President

557. Hello _____, Hello _____

558. _____Don't You Walk So Fast

POINTS:

THE GUESS WHO!

559.

A. I led a group called the Flying Machine before I found stardom as a solo soft-rock artist.

B. My sister Kate and my brother Livingston also recorded albums.

C. My wife is also a rock star—Carly Simon.

I am?   Points:

560.

A. I was a rock star who died in a plane crash.

B. I sang with my wife Ingrid before I became a big solo hit.

C. I sang about a guy on the South Side of Chicago.

My name was?   Points:

561.

A. I was once a member of the Lovin' Spoonful.

B. I quit the Spoonful but was not as successful in my solo career.

C. The public said "Welcome Back" when I had a number-one song in 1976.

My name is?   Points:

562.

A. I am a singer-songwriter from Brooklyn, New York.

B. I was a star in the early 60's and made a successful comeback in the mid-70's.

C. I had hit records twice with "Breaking Up Is Hard to Do."

I am?   Points:

Identify these singers after Clue A for 5 points, after Clue B for 3 points, and after Clue C for 1 point.

563.

A. I am a singer hailing from Philadelphia, Pennsylvania.

B. I had a 1976 hit with a disco version of "Venus."

C. I co-starred in countless beach movies with Annette Funicello.

My name is?   Points:

564.

A. I am a country singer who had a bushel of pop hits in the mid-60's.

B. I had a short-lived variety series on NBC.

C. Even though I'm "King of the Road," you can "Dang Me."

I am?   Points:

565.

A. I was musical director for Bette Midler.

B. I wrote the jingles for McDonald's and State Farm Insurance.

C. "I Write the Songs" like "Mandy" and "Could It Be Magic?"

My name is?   Points:

566.

A. I am a black, blind soul singer.

B. I'm not Stevie Wonder.

C. My career has stretched from the early 50's to the present, and my hits include "What I Say" and "Unchain My Heart."

I am?   Points:

567.

A. I am one of the best known rockers of the 50's.

B. My trademark is doing the duck walk while I play the guitar.

C. While my songs have been recorded by the Beatles, the Rolling Stones, and the Beach Boys, my first number-one song was "My Ding-a-Ling" in 1972.

My name is?   Points:

568.

A. I was a member of the Mamas and the Papas.

B. After the group split, I "Made My Own Kind of Music" and teamed up with Dave Mason.

C. And no one's getting fat 'cept . . . me.

My name was?   Points:

Total Points:

Re-Recorded!

Over the years, many songs have been recorded by more than one singer or group. We'll provide a list of hitmakers, you take that list and name as many singers as you can who had a hit with each of the following songs for one point each. Some of the singers will be used more than once, so be careful!

The Beatles, Ringo Starr, John Lennon, the Beach Boys, the Who, the Bay City Rollers, the Doors, Cat Stevens, Ike and Tina Turner, Creedence Clearwater Revival, the Tremeloes, Ben E. King, Little Eva, the Mamas and the Papas, Chuck Berry, Harold Dorman, the Everly Brothers, the Dave Clark Five, José Feliciano, Gladys Knight and the Pips, Eddie Cochran, Linda Ronstadt, Sam Cooke, Johnny Rivers, Grand Funk Railroad, the Four Seasons, Joey Dee and the Starliters, Bette Midler, Marvin Gaye, Dusty Springfield, Dale Hawkins, the Platters, the Contours, Herman's Hermits, Bobby Freeman, Anne Murray, Spider Turner, the Isley Brothers, and Blue Cheer.

569.	I Heard It Through The Grapevine (3)
570.	The Locomotion (2)
571.	Do You Wanna Dance? (4)
572.	Do You Love Me? (2)
573.	Summertime Blues (3)
574.	Rock and Roll Music (3)
575.	Silence Is Golden (2)
576.	Another Saturday Night (2)
577.	Proud Mary (2)
578.	Stand By Me (3)
579.	I Only Want to Be with You (2)
580.	You Won't See Me (2)

581.	Mountain of Love (2)
582.	Only You (2)
583.	When Will I Be Loved? (2)
584.	Shout (2)
585.	Wonderful World (2)
586.	Susie Q (2)
587.	Light My Fire (2)
POINTS:	

Take Me to Your Leader!

Name the lead singer of each group for one point.

588.	589.	590.	591.
THE LOVIN' SPOONFUL	THE FIVE SATINS	BREAD	THE RONETTES
592.	**593.**	**594.**	**595.**
THEM	THE WHO	THE GUESS WHO	NAZZ
596.	**597.**	**598.**	**599.**
THE CRESTS	CREEDENCE CLEARWATER REVIVAL	THE MIRACLES	THE SPENCER DAVIS GROUP
600.	**601.**	**602.**	**603.**
THE CLASSICS IV	THE RASPBERRIES	THE DOORS	THE FOUR TOPS
604.	**605.**	**606.**	**607.**
HARVEY AND THE MOONGLOWS	THE BYRDS	THE PLATTERS	THE SKYLINERS
608.	**609.**	**610.**	**Points:**
FREE	JAY AND THE AMERICANS	THE JACKSON FIVE	

The People's Choice!

614. Gimme Some Lovin'
- a. The Fifth Dimension
- b. Barry White
- c. Bruce Springsteen
- d. The Spencer Davis Group
- e. The Buddy Miles Express

615. Come Go with Me
- a. The Earls
- b. Lloyd Price
- c. The Dell-Vikings
- d. The Diamonds
- e. The Andrea True Connection

616. Build Me Up, Buttercup
- a. Edison Lighthouse
- b. The Spiral Starecase
- c. The Buckinghams
- d. The Foundations
- e. Hamilton, Joe Frank and Reynolds

611. Keep on Dancing
- a. The Gentrys
- b. The Grass Roots
- c. Leo Sayer
- d. Steppenwolf
- e. Chris Montez

617. Follow the Boys
- a. Lesley Gore
- b. Connie Francis
- c. Brenda Lee
- d. David Bowie
- e. Elton John

612. Image of a Girl
- a. Billy J. Kramer and the Dakotas
- b. Patti Smith
- c. The Safaris
- d. The Surfaris
- e. The Friends of Distinction

618. It Hurts to Be in Love
- a. Dr. Hook and the Medicine Show
- b. Dr. Feelgood and the Interns
- c. Gene Pitney
- d. The Essex
- e. Bobby Rydell

613. I Wonder What She's Doing Tonight
- a. Glen Campbell
- b. Mac Davis
- c. Sonny and Cher
- d. The Allman Brothers Band
- e. Barry and the Tamerlanes

619. Little Star
- a. Kathy Young and the Innocents
- b. Zager and Evans
- c. Crispian St. Peter
- d. The Elegants
- e. Mickey Rooney

Pick the singer or group who had the following hits for one point each. **Points:**

What Kind of Fool Am I?

620. *Match the singer with the foolish song for one point each.*

Fools Rush In	Connie Francis
Poor Little Fool	The Beatles
Everybody's Somebody's Fool	The Tams
Fool on the Hill	Frankie Lymon and the Teenagers
Foolish Little Girl	Brook Benton
What Kind of Fool Do You Think I Am?	The Shirelles
What Kind of Fool Am I?	Ricky Nelson
Why Do Fools Fall in Love?	Sammy Davis, Jr.

Points: _____

THE NAME GAME!

Many song titles have boy's names in them, too. Fill in the correct male name for one point each.

621. Message to _____ by Dionne Warwick

622. _____ by Sue Thompson

623. Sloop _____ B. by the Beach Boys

624. _____'s Girl by Marcie Blane

625. Me and _____ McGee by Janis Joplin

626. _____ Angel by Shelley Fabares

627. I'm _____ VIII (I Am) by Herman's Hermits

628. _____ B. Goode by Chuck Berry

629. _____ the Red-Nosed Reindeer by Gene Autry

630. _____'s Harmonica by the Chipmunks

631. _____ My Love by the Teen Queens

632. _____ (Row the Boat Ashore) by the Highwaymen

633. _____ Raccoon by the Beatles

634. The Ballad of Bungalow _____ by the Beatles

635. Ode to _____ by Bobbie Gentry

636. Hats Off to _____ by Del Shannon

637. Hit the Road _____ by Ray Charles

638. _____ by Abba

639. Big Bad _____ by Jimmy Dean

640. Do the _____ by Freddie and the Dreamers

641. Duke of _____ by Gene Chandler

642. _____, _____ by the Kingsmen

643. Killer _____ by the Rocky Fellers

644. _____ by Reparata and the Delrons

645. I Love _____ by Teresa Brewer

646. Me and _____ Down by the Schoolyard by Paul Simon

647. _____ the Italian Mouse by Lou Monte

648. Ragtime Cowboy _____ by the Chipmunks

649. _____ the Knife by Bobby Darin

650. Brother _____ by Stories

651. _____ Brown by the Coasters

652. Tall _____ by Annette

653. _____ Dandy by LaVern Baker

654. I Was Kaiser _____'s Batman by Whistlin' Jack Smith

655. Stagger _____ by Lloyd Price

656. The Ballad of _____ Crockett by Fess Parker

657. _____ Jingo by Hayley Mills

658. _____ Gunn Theme by Henry Mancini

659. _____'s Monkey by the Miracles

660. Down at Papa _____'s by the Dixiebelles

661. Hey _____(Your Mama's Callin') by Jimmy Castor

662. _____ Get Angry by Joanie Sommers

663. _____ the Hairy Ape by Ray Stevens

664. _____ the Arab by Ray Stevens

665. Hey _____ by the Leaves or by Jimi Hendrix

666. _____ by Dionne Warwick

667. Which Way You Goin' _____? by the Poppy Family

668. _____ Dooley by the Kingston Trio

669. Tale of the _____ Fitzgerald by Gordon Lightfoot

670. _____ by the Buoys

671. _____ Don't Be a Hero by Bo Donaldson and the Heywoods

672. Hey _____ by the Beatles

673. The Ballad of _____ and Yoko by the Beatles

674. _____ and the Jets by Elton John

675. Dance with Me _____ by Georgia Gibbs

Points: _____

FUN, FUN, FUN
IN THE PARKIN' LOT
POM POM PLAY GIRL · THIS CAR
OF MINE · SHUT DOWN, PART II
CASSIUS LOVE vs. SONNY WILSON

SHUT
DOWN
VOLUME 2

WHY DO FOOLS FALL IN LOVE
THE WARMTH OF THE SUN
DON'T WORRY BABY
DENNY'S DRUMS · LOUIE LOUIE
KEEP AN EYE ON SUMMER

the beach boys

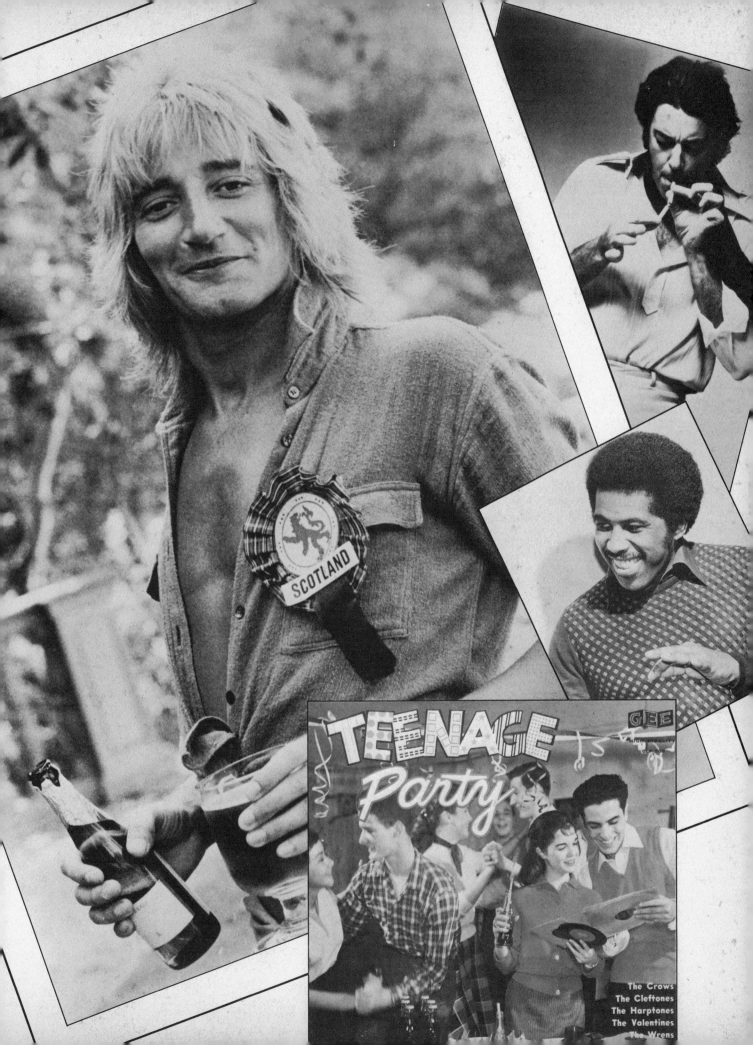

SCOTLAND

TEENAGE
Party

GEE

The Crows
The Cleftones
The Harptones
The Valentines
The Wrens

a.	Rain		The Guess Who
b.	Raindrops		Lou Christie
c.	In the Rain		The Cowsills
d.	Laughter in the Rain		The Temptations
e.	Walking in the Rain		Glenn Yarborough
f.	Walking in the Rain with the One I Love		Brook Benton
g.	Rhapsody in the Rain		The Beatles
h.	Rhythm of the Rain		Creedence Clearwater Revival
i.	The Rain, the Park and Other Things		Neil Sedaka
j.	Rain on the Roof		Love Unlimited
k.	Who'll Stop the Rain?		Bob Dylan
l.	Raindrops Keep Falling on My Head		Buddy Holly
m.	Baby, the Rain Must Fall		Creedence Clearwater Revival
n.	I Wish That It Would Rain		The Dramatics
o.	Raining in My Heart		The Cascades
p.	Have You Ever Seen the Rain?		Dee Clark
q.	Raindance		The Lovin' Spoonful
r.	A Rainy Night in Georgia		The Ronettes
s.	Rainy Day Women #12 and #35		B. J. Thomas
t.	Hey, Rainy Jane		The Critters
u.	Here Comes That Rainy Day Feelin' Again		The Fortunes
v.	Rainy Day Man		Davy Jones
w.	Don't Let the Rain Fall Down on Me		James Taylor
POINTS:			

676. *Every Cloud Has a Silver Lining . . . or a Gold Record!*

Into every life a little rain must fall, especially if you listen to the radio. Your mission, should you decide to accept it, is to match the rainy rock to the singers for one point each!

The Gang's all Here!

Name the members of the following groups. You get one point for every group you correctly name.

677. Name the four singers who made up the **Mamas and the Papas.** _____

678. Identify the four **Young Rascals.** _____

679. Who are the four people composing the **Who?** _____

680. Name the three **Chipmunks** and their leader. _____

681. Give the names of the original five **Beach Boys.** _____

682. What four musicians made up the **Doors?** _____

683. Who are **Three Dog Night?** _____

684. Name the three members of **Cream.** _____

685. Identify the current members of **Fleetwood Mac.** _____

686. Who are the three **Bee Gees?** _____

687. Name the original five **Rolling Stones.** _____

688. Identify the two **Righteous Brothers.** _____

689. What four musicians were known as **Blind Faith?** _____

690. Who were the original **Four Seasons?** _____

691. Name the four original **Monkees.** _____

692. Identify the four members of the **Manhattan Transfer.** _____

Points: _____

Executive

S U I T E !

Not all the superstars in the music business are the
ones with their voices on the records. Some
of the real superstars sit behind desks. They sign
talent, promote records, and sometimes produce a
unique sound all their own. In this salute to
the men and women behind the music, match the
record executive with the record label
he or she is associated with.
Score one point for each correct answer.

**Lou Adler, Herb Alpert, Neil Bogart, Clive Davis,
Ahmet Ertegun, David Geffen,
Berry Gordy, Florence Greenberg, Sam Phillips,
Phil Spector**

Scepter

Atlantic

Casablanca

A&M

Motown

Ode

Columbia (Arista)

Sun

Asylum

Phillies

693.

POINTS:

694. Hard-hitting political songs were the spearhead of much rock 'n' roll in the 60's and early 70's. Which of the following songs is probably *not* considered to be political in nature?   a. The Eve of Destruction   b. Blowin' in the Wind   c. Ohio   d. Give Peace a Chance   e. We Shall Overcome   f. Disco Duck

695. Which of the following television stars never recorded a 45-rpm record?   a. Jerry "Beaver" Mathers   b. Johnny Crawford   c. Lorne Greene   d. Ken "Eddie Haskell" Osmond   e. Annette Funicello   f. Paul Peterson   g. Shelley Fabares   h. John Travolta   i. Walter Brennan   j. Fess Parker

696. Which of the following TV show theme songs was never released as a 45-rpm record?   a. Secret Agent   b. Batman   c. Route 66   d. Hawaii Five-O   e. The Midnight Special   f. All in the Family   g. Happy Days   h. Welcome Back (Kotter)   i. Laverne and Shirley (We're Gonna Make Our Dreams Come True)   j. The Fugitive   k. Zorro   l. The Rockford Files   m. Baretta

697. Name the artist who performed each of these different songs: a. Somebody to Love (1967 version)   b. Somebody to Love (1977 version)   c. To Love Somebody   d. Tonight's the Night (c. 1962)   e. Tonight's the Night (c. 1976)

698. Fill in the correct day of the week in these song titles:

a. I've Got _____ On Mind by the Easy Beats

b. Ruby _____ by the Rolling Stones

c. _____ Will Never Be the Same by Spanky and Our Gang

d. _____ Night's Alright for Fightin by Elton John

e. _____, _____ by the Mamas and the Papas

699. What was the original name of the group Chicago?

700. Which of these records was never a hit for the Bee Gees: a. Gotta Get a Message to You   b. You Should Be Dancing   c. I Started a Joke   d. I Started a Fire   e. Jive Talkin'

701. Cream had hits like "Sunshine of Your Love" and "White Room." They also had some big-selling albums. Which of the following was not the title of a Cream album: a. Disraeli Gears   b. Fresh Cream   c. Crop of the Cream   d. Wheels of Fire   e. Good-Bye   f. Cream, Cheese, and Bagels

Give yourself one point for every correct answer to these questions.   **Points:** _____

𝒫OTPOURRI FOR THE EXPERT!

Sons of the Beach!

The crash of the surf on the beach, blond musclemen carrying surfboards, sun-drenched beach bunnies in bikinis—these were all a big part of the music of the 60's. But we could never figure out why surf music was so big in the Midwest, where the nearest ocean was a thousand miles away and a wave was something you did when you said goodbye. Anyway, give yourself one point for every correct answer to these questions on the Beach Boys and other surfing groups.

POINTS: _____

702. The Beach Boys wish that all girls could be "California Girls"—which would mean that boys from New Jersey would have to drive three thousand miles to pick up their dates. What did the Beach Boys like about girls from the North, South, East and Midwest?

_____

703. The Beach Boys based "Surfin' USA" on what Chuck Berry song?

_____

704. Which one of these musicians was never a Beach Boy: a. Glen Campbell b. "Captain" Darryl Dragon c. Blondie Chaplin d. Bruce Johnston e. Ricky Fataar f. Al Jardine g. Al Jolson

_____

705. Who is Murray Wilson?

_____

706. The Beach Boys split with Capitol Records in the late 60's over forming their own record company. What is the name of the record company the Beach Boys finally formed?

_____

707. Which of these songs was *not* a Beach Boys single: a. Wild Honey b. Sail On Sailor c. Heroes and Villains d. Add Some Music to Your Day e. Suzie Cincinnati f. I Sunburned My Armpits on Redondo Beach g. 409

_____

708. She'll have "Fun, Fun, Fun" until what cataclysmic event takes place?

_____

709. What classic Beach Boys album contained "Sloop John B," "Wouldn't It Be Nice," "God Only Knows," and "Caroline No"?

_____

710. What Beach Boys album first featured the song "Good Vibrations"?

_____

_____

711. What has a first gear that's all right, a second gear that makes you lean right, and a third gear that makes you hang on tight?

_____

_____

712. Mike Love and Brian Wilson wrote that song, and the Beach Boys did record it, but who had the hit with it?

_____

_____

713. Who did the Beach Boys need help from?

_____

_____

714. In 1972, the Beach Boys recorded an album in a foreign land and named it after that country. What is the name of that album?

_____

_____

715. Jan and Dean were long-time buddies of the Beach Boys. Do they have last names?

_____

_____

716. The Rivieras had a hit with "California Sun." Who was their lead singer?

_____

_____

717. During the 60's, every drummer in every high school band had to show his drumming prowess by playing "Wipe Out" at every high school dance. Who had the hit with "Wipe Out"?

_____

_____

718. Match the following songs to the group who recorded them:

Little GTO	Jan and Dean
Little Deuce Coupe	The Ventures
Drag City	Ronnie and the Daytonas
Hey Little Cobra	The Beach Boys
Walk, Don't Run	The Ripchords

There have been many rock 'n' roll songs celebrating states of the United States. Name the artists who performed these state songs for one point each.

719.	Kentucky Woman
720.	Kentucky Rain
721.	Hawaii Five-0
722.	North to Alaska
723.	Indiana Wants Me
724.	Arizona
725.	The Yellow Rose of Texas
726.	Ohio
727.	Massachusetts
728.	Sweet Home Alabama
729.	Georgia
730.	Georgia on My Mind
731.	Midnight Train to Georgia
732.	A Rainy Night in Georgia
733.	The Night the Lights Went Out in Georgia
734.	California Dreaming
735.	California Nights
736.	California Sun
737.	California Girls
738.	The Only Living Boy in New York

BONUS: Name the artists of these country songs for one point each!

739.	Brazil
740.	England Swings
741.	Little Egypt
742.	Back in the USSR
743.	Living in the USA

I'm a Travelin' Man!

Points:

♪BODY LANGUAGE!

Name the parts of the body found in these song titles for one point each.

744. _____ Poppin' Time

745. Back in My _____ Again

746. I Want to Hold Your _____

747. Goin' Out of My _____

748. I Only Have _____ for You

749. Wear My Ring Around Your _____

750. _____ And Soul

751. She Lets Her _____ Down

752. Put Your _____ in the _____

753. Beauty's Only _____ Deep

754. Put Your _____ on My _____

755. Love Is Like an Itching in My _____

756. These _____

757. Wooden _____

758. My Boyfriend's _____

POINTS:

♪Croon the Tune, Then Place The Face!

Here are the songs, now name the artist for one point each.

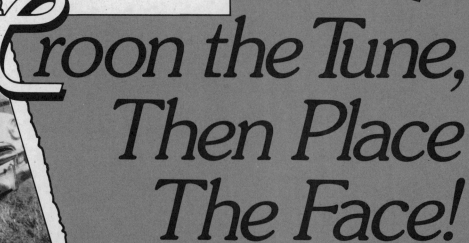

759.

"What'd I Say," "I Can't Stop Loving You," and "Unchain My Heart"

760.

"I Think We're Alone Now," "Crystal Blue Persuasion," and "Mony Mony"

761.

"I Know A Place," "Don't Sleep in the Subway, Darling," and "Love This Is My Song"

762.

"Chain Gang," "Twistin' the Night Away," and "You Send Me"

763.

"Ain't That a Shame," "I Hear You Knockin'," and "I'm Walkin'"

764.

"Dream Lover," "Splish Splash," and "Mack the Knife"

765.

"All I Have to Do Is Dream," "Bye Bye Love," and "Cathy's Clown"

766.

"How Can I Be Sure?," "Good Lovin'," and "Groovin'"

767.

"It's Only Rock and Roll (But I Like It)," "Time Is On My Side," and "Let's Spend the Night Together"

768.

"Brother Love's Traveling Salvation Show," "Girl, You'll Be a Woman Soon," and "Soolaimon"

769.

"Positively Fourth Street," "Like a Rolling Stone," and "Lay Lady Lay"

770.

"The Boxer," "My Little Town," and "I Am a Rock"

771.

"New Kid in Town," "Lyin' Eyes," and "Take it Easy"

772.

"Wear Your Love Like Heaven," "Atlantis," and "Sunshine Superman"

773.

"I've Been Searchin' So Long," "If You Leave Me Now," and "Saturday in the Park"

TOTAL POINTS:

The Guess Who-Part Two!

Identify these singers after Clue A and win 5 points, after Clue B for 3 points, and after Clue C for 1 point.

774.	A.	I replaced Clyde McPhatter as lead singer for the Drifters.
	B.	When I left the Drifters, I sang about "Spanish Harlem."
	C.	I made a comeback in 1976 with "Supernatural Thing."
	My name is?	**Points:**
775.	A.	I was once a member of Buffalo Springfield.
	B.	I then joined a group that hit it big with "Marrakesh Express."
	C.	I had no hit song with Super Session, but I did well solo with "Love the One You're With."
	I am?	**Points:**
776.	A.	First they took our song and made it the theme of the movie *Blackboard Jungle*.
	B.	Then they took our song and made it the theme of a movie with the same title.
	C.	Then they took our song and made it the original theme of the TV show *Happy Days*.
	We are?	**Points:**
777.	A.	Remember that *Every Picture Tells a Story*.
	B.	You might have heard me singing "I Know I'm Losing You" to Britt Ekland.
	C.	"Maggie Mae," but Dora Does and Wanda Will!
	My name is?	**Points:**
778.	A.	I was in the back-up group for Ricky Nelson.
	B.	Then I was in the group Gary Lewis and the Playboys.
	C.	I've done solo work since and also was a stalwart of Joe Cocker's Mad Dogs and Englishmen.
	I am?	**Points:**
	TOTAL POINTS:	

Number Please!

Each of these song titles has a number in it.
Fill in the correct number for one point each.

779. Love Potion Number _____

780. A _____ to _____

781. _____ Candles

782. Happy Birthday Sweet _____

783. _____ Ways to Leave Your Lover

784. The Night has _____ Eyes

785. _____ Tears

786. Knock _____ Times

787. _____ Summer Night

788. Route _____ Theme

789. _____ O'Clock World

790. A Quarter to _____

791. _____ Reasons

792. Never in a _____ Years

793. _____ Nervous Breakdown

794. Beechwood _____

795. _____ Pounds of Clay

796. You're _____ (You're Beautiful and You're Mine)

797. _____ Miles (across the Sea)

798. _____ Miles (to Go)

799. A _____ Miles Away

800. I'm Henry _____

801. _____ Commandments of Love

802. _____ or _____ to _____ by Chicago

803. Opus _____

804. _____ Stars in the Sky

805. _____ Little Girls Sitting in the Back Seat

806. Questions _____ and _____

807. The _____ Bells

808. _____ - _____ - _____ by Len Barry

809. _____ Track Mind

810. Engine Engine Number _____

811. _____ Rooms of Gloom

812. Land of _____ Dances

813. _____ (Is the Loneliest Number)

POINTS: _____

95

Devil or Angel!

814.	DEVIL OR ANGEL
a.	Bobby Vinton
b.	The Clovers
c.	Sam Cooke
d.	Bobby Vee
e.	Gene Pitney

815.	DEVIL IN DISGUISE
a.	Ral Donner
b.	John Fred and his Playboy Band
c.	Elvis Presley
d.	Freddie Scott
e.	Dion

816.	DEVIL WITH A BLUE DRESS ON
a.	The Young Rascals
b.	Mitch Ryder and the Detroit Wheels
c.	The Lovin' Spoonful
d.	Bill Haley and the Comets
e.	Blood, Sweat and Tears

817.	DEVIL WOMAN
a.	Cliff Richards
b.	Santana
c.	Donovan
d.	Electric Light Orchestra
e.	Canned Heat

818.	SYMPATHY FOR THE DEVIL
a.	Grand Funk Railroad
b.	Kiss
c.	Screamin' Jay Hawkins
d.	Malo
e.	The Rolling Stones

819.	ANGEL OF THE MORNING
a.	The Poppy Family
b.	Marianne Faithfull
c.	Merilee Rush
d.	Linda Ronstadt
e.	Abba

820.	EARTH ANGEL
a.	The Mello-Kings
b.	The Penguins
c.	The Five Satins
d.	The Spaniels
e.	The Crows

821.	JOHNNY ANGEL
a.	Shelley Fabares
b.	Annette
c.	Marcie Blane
d.	Little Peggy March
e.	Labelle

822.	NEXT DOOR TO AN ANGEL
a.	Paul Anka
b.	Frankie Avalon
c.	Fabian
d.	Jerry Butler
e.	Neil Sedaka

Select the correct singer or group having a hit with these songs about devils and angels for one point each.

823.	THE ANGELS LISTENED IN
	a. The Earls
	b. The Crests
	c. The Brooklyn Bridge
	d. The Exciters
	e. The Dubs
824.	MY SPECIAL ANGEL
	a. The Bachelors
	b. The Classics IV
	c. The Vogues
	d. The Carpenters
	e. Andy Williams
825.	PRETTY LITTLE ANGEL EYES
	a. Thurston Harris
	b. Bobby Day
	c. Curtis Lee
	d. Bobby Freeman
	e. Kinky Friedman
826.	TEEN ANGEL
	a. Mark Dinning
	b. Ray Peterson
	c. The Nutmegs
	d. Del Shannon
	e. J. Frank Wilson and the Cavaliers
827.	BLUE ANGEL
	a. Jerry Lee Lewis
	b. Burl Ives
	c. The Marcels
	d. Roy Orbison
	e. Marlene Dietrich
828.	LONELY NIGHTS (ANGEL FACE)
	a. Maxine Nightingale
	b. Sonny and Cher
	c. The Bee Gees
	d. Aretha Franklin
	e. The Captain and Tennille

POINTS:

KNOW YOUR BASIC FOOD GROUPS!

You get one point for each group or singer you can remember that has a food or flavor in its name. We'll give you a hit song they had, you name the nourishing artist!

829. Go All the Way _____

830. Green Tambourine _____

831. You Sexy Thing _____

832. You Keep Me Hanging On _____

833. For Your Love _____

834. Pachalafaka _____

835. Incense and Peppermints _____

836. Will You Be Staying after Sunday? _____

837. Don't Say Nothing Bad about My Baby _____

838. Daddy's Home _____

POINTS:

THE SUPREMES
A BIT
OF
LIVERPOOL

A HARD DAYS NIGHT
HOUSE OF THE RISING SUN
BITS AND PIECES
I WANT TO HOLD YOUR HAND
CAN'T BUY ME LOVE
YOU'VE REALLY GOT A HOLD ON ME
YOU CAN'T DO THAT
DO YOU LOVE ME
HOW DO YOU DO IT
WORLD WITHOUT LOVE
BECAUSE

Peter Paul and Mary
IN THE WIND

IT'S ONLY WORDS!

Answer these questions based on lyrics of favorite songs for one point each.

839. In "Ode to Billy Joe," what day of the year was another "dusty delta day"?

_____

_____

840. In "Only in America," Jay and the Americans told us that   a. the poorest person could go to sleep and wake up a

_____ , and
b. a child without a cent could grow up to be

_____

841. What is waiting for me "twenty-six miles across the sea"?

_____

_____

842. In "The Name Game," which of these names was not used: a. Lincoln   b. Shirley
c. Marsha   d. Nick   e. Chuck

_____

_____

843. In what dramatic song does the artist triumphantly proclaim that a dollar is a dollar and a dime is a dime?

_____

_____

844. In "You Light Up My Life," what do you give me in order to let me carry on?

_____

_____

845. Fill in the names of the campers from Allan Sherman's "Hello Muddah, Hello Faddah":

a. _____ (He developed poison ivy)

b. _____ (He got ptomaine poisoning last night after dinner)

c. _____ (They're about to organize a searching party)

d. SPECIAL—5 extra trivia points for naming the aunt whom he would even let hug and kiss him.

_____

846. In "King of the Road," how much were rooms to let?

_____

847. In "Rock around the Clock," where will we be when the clock strikes five, six, and seven?

_____

848. For one point each, list the five names used in the song "Fifty Ways to Leave Your Lover."

_____

849. For one point each, name the four chapters in "The Book of Love."
1)   3)
2)   4)

850. Remember the guy who hated to leave you, but he really felt he must say . . . what?

_____

851. In the song "Love Potion No. 9," where did he kiss a cop?

_____

_____

852. In its pure, undiluted form, what substances did "Love Potion No. 9" resemble?

_____

_____

853. Last night he went for a walk in the dark at what former famous, but greasy, amusement park? (ten extra trivia points for knowing who wrote the song.)

_____

Points:

A Near Ms.!

854. In this age of the liberated woman, we would be re-ms. in forgetting the contributions of female rock 'n' roll groups. Match the girl group to the song for one point each.

a.	He's A Rebel		The Bobbettes
b.	Be My Baby		Rosie and the Originals
c.	Remember (Walking in the Sand)		Reparata and the Delrons
d.	My Boyfriend's Back		The Ronettes
e.	One Fine Day		The Chordettes
f.	Whenever a Teenager Cries		The Shirelles
g.	Angel Baby		The Crystals
h.	Maybe		The Poni-Tails
i.	Will You Love Me Tomorrow?		The Angels
j.	Please Don't Kiss Me Again		The Shangri-Las
k.	Mr. Sandman		Merci
l.	Mr. Lee		The Jaynettes
m.	Sally Go Round the Roses		The Charmettes
n.	Love Will Make You Happy		The Chiffons
o.	Born Too Late		The Chantels
Points:			

855. Please Come to Boston _____

856. The Boy from New York City _____

857. Coney Island Baby _____

858. Spanish Harlem _____

859. Wildwood Days _____

860. Philadelphia Freedom _____

861. The Sound of Philadelphia (TSOP) _____

862. Goodbye Columbus _____

863. Detroit City _____

864. The Night Chicago Died _____

865. Nashville Cats _____

866. Memphis _____

867. Tallahassee Lassie _____

868. New Orleans _____

869. City of New Orleans _____

870. Walkin' to New Orleans _____

871. Battle of New Orleans _____

872. Way Down Yonder in New Orleans _____

873. Kansas City _____

874. Wichita Lineman _____

875. El Paso _____

876. By the Time I Get to Phoenix _____

877. L.A. Woman _____

878. Hollywood Swingin' _____

879. Little Old Lady from Pasadena _____

880. Do You Know the Way to San Jose? _____

881. San Francisco (Wear Some Flowers in Your Hair) _____

882. San Franciscan Nights _____

883. Seattle _____

884. Honolulu Lulu _____ **POINTS:**

They're Really Rockin' in Boston, Pittsburgh, Pa.!

Rock and roll has traveled from coast to coast and border to border. Sit back as we travel from the East Coast to the West and identify the singer promoting each city we pass through for one point.

WOODSTOCK!

Write yes next to the name of anyone you think performed at the rock festival; write no if not. Each correct answer is worth one point.

	885.	Canned Heat
	886.	Melanie
	887.	Joni Mitchell
	888.	John Sebastian
	889.	Country Joe and the Fish
	890.	The Allman Brothers Band
	891.	The Rolling Stones
	892.	Richie Havens
	893.	Arlo Guthrie
	894.	Joan Baez
	895.	Sha Na Na
	896.	Iron Butterfly
	897.	Led Zeppelin
	898.	Crosby, Stills and Nash
	899.	The Who
	900.	The Guess Who
	901.	Joe Cocker
	902.	Santana
	903.	Spirit
	904.	Ten Years After
	905.	The Moody Blues
	906.	The Butterfield Blues Band
	907.	Jefferson Airplane
	908.	Procol Harum
	909.	Sly and the Family Stone
	910.	Steppenwolf
	911.	Jethro Tull
	912.	Jimi Hendrix
	913.	The Beatles

POINTS:

The British Are Coming!

Starting in 1964, British rock groups invaded America, ushering in a new sound. Each of these questions is worth one point.

914. The Searchers—one of the first of the British groups to strike gold in America—sang, "I had to get down on my knees and pray." But soon it begins. What begins?

_____

_____

915. Which of the following songs was not a hit for the Kinks? a. Lola   b. A Well Respected Man   c. You Really Got Me   d. Love Potion No. 9   e. All Day and All of the Night   f. Tired of Waiting for You

_____

_____

916. Gerry and the Pacemakers warned "Don't Let the Sun Catch You Crying"! One way to prevent this was suggested in another of their songs. Which river did they advise us to cross?

_____

_____

103

917. "For Your Love" was a hit by:
a. The Byrds   b. The Yardbirds   c. Cindy Birdsong   d. Led Zeppelin   e. Eagles

918. Which group may have said to their girlfriends, "I'm Telling You Now That You Were Made for Me!":   a. Bay City Rollers
b. Herman's Hermits   c. Manfred Mann
d. Freddie and the Dreamers   e. The Zombies

919. What hit song was on the flip-side of Herman's Hermits' hit "There's a Kind of Hush"?

920. Herman's Hermits lead singer, Peter Noone, announced "I'm into Something Good." Mick Jagger of the Rolling Stones was less lucky and complained "I Can't Get No

921. What British group had hits with "Bus Stop," "Stop, Stop, Stop," and "Long Cool Woman in a Black Dress"?

922. Match the group to the hit:
a. The Zombies   __I'm Crying
b. Led Zeppelin   __Pinball Wizard
c. The Who   __Little Children
d. The Animals   __Whole Lotta Love
e. Billy J. Kramer and the   __She's Not There
   Dakotas

923. In the rock opera *Tommy,* what was the name of Tommy's wicked uncle?   a. Uncle Bernard   b. Uncle Phil   c. Uncle Ernie   d. Uncle Joe   e. Uncle Al   f. Uncle Danny   g. Uncle Abe   h. Uncle Irv   i. Uncle Jack   j. Uncle Nutsy

924. Arrange these statements in the correct order: a. Touch Me   b. Heal Me   c. See Me   d. Feel Me

925. When critics claimed that their first song lacked relevance, with a frivolous title like "Doo Wah Diddy Diddy," Manfred Mann came back with a hit called what?

926. What has been the ruin of many a poor boy in New Orleans?

927. Many of us sang this Animals song in high school as the day dragged on and on and on. What song do you suppose it was?

928. Peter and Gordon wanted to be locked away. Where didn't they want to stay under any circumstances?

929. Who teased "Catch Us If You Can"?

930. Which song was the Moody Blues' first hit in America?   a. Ride My See-Saw   b. Nights in White Satin   c. Go Now   d. Tuesday Afternoon   e. I'm Just a Singer in a Rock and Roll Band

931. In "I'm Henry VIII, I Am," how many times has the widow next door been married?

932. In "Honky Tonk Woman," where did Mick Jagger meet a "gin-soaked barroom queen"?

933. True or false? The Nashville Teens, who had a hit with the song "Tobacco Road," were really from England.

P O I N T S :

DO YOU BELIEVE IN MAGIC?

Match the "magical" song to the group that turned it into a hit for one point each.

934.	This Magic Moment	Bobby Darin
935.	Magic Carpet Ride	Santana
936.	Magic Man	The Electric Light Orchestra
937.	Black Magic Woman	The Lovin' Spoonful
938.	That Old Black Magic	Steppenwolf
939.	Magical Mystery Tour	The Bay City Rollers
940.	It's Magic	Barry Manilow
941.	Puff the Magic Dragon	Heart
942.	Strange Magic	The Dubs
943.	My Baby Must Be a Magician	The Drifters/Jay and the Americans
944.	Could This Be Magic?	Peter, Paul and Mary
945.	Could It Be Magic?	Pilot
946.	Do You Believe in Magic?	The Marvelettes
947.	You Made Me Believe in Magic	The Beatles
		Points:

Boys and Girls Together!

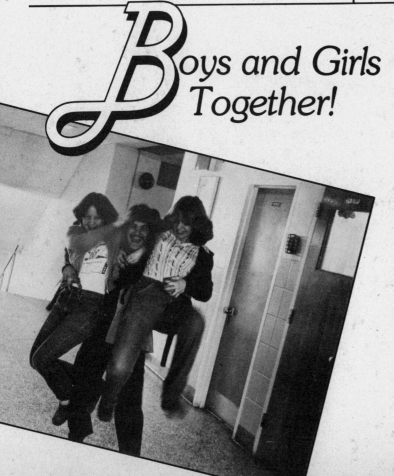

For one point each tell us whether these swinging groups were boy groups, girl groups, or boys and girls together.

948. Fleetwood Mac _____

949. The Five Satins _____

950. Abba _____

951. The Crystals _____

952. The Orlons _____

953. The Association _____

954. The Drifters _____

955. The Platters _____

956. Fanny _____

957. The Hollies _____

958. Jefferson Starship _____

959. The Brooklyn Bridge _____

Points: _____

March of the Horribles!

960. *Match the horror novelty song to the person, group, or thing that recorded it for 5 points each!!!*

a.	THE MUMMY		Nervous Norvus
b.	THE CREATURE		Fats Domino
c.	THE BLOB		Randy Fuller
d.	THE WITCH DOCTOR		Gene and Wendell
e.	THE MARTIAN HOP		Bubi and Bob
f.	DINNER WITH DRAC		Sheb Wooley
g.	WEREWOLF		Phil Harris
h.	WOLFMAN		Buchanan and Ancell
i.	MONSTER MASH		Zacherle
j.	MONSTER ROCK 'N' ROLL		The Five Blobs
k.	THE ROACH		The Randells
l.	HAUNTED HOUSE		The Frantics
m.	THE THING		David Seville
n.	THE FANG		Jumpin' Gene Simmons
o.	THE PURPLE PEOPLE EATER		Bobby "Boris" Pickett
Points:			

In the early days of rock 'n' roll, critics called the music "animalistic." Since we don't take such criticism lightly, we decided to give you a list of animalistic songs. Fill in the blanks with the animals of your choice, and if your choice happens to be correct, give yourself one point.

POINTS:

961. _____ Love

962. Lucky _____ and the _____

963. The _____ Walk

964. Running _____

965. Baby _____ Time

966. The Lonely _____ Train

967. Mickey's _____ Sleeps Tonight

968. _____ Man

969. The _____ by the Everly Brothers

970. Disco _____

971. _____

972. _____

973. _____

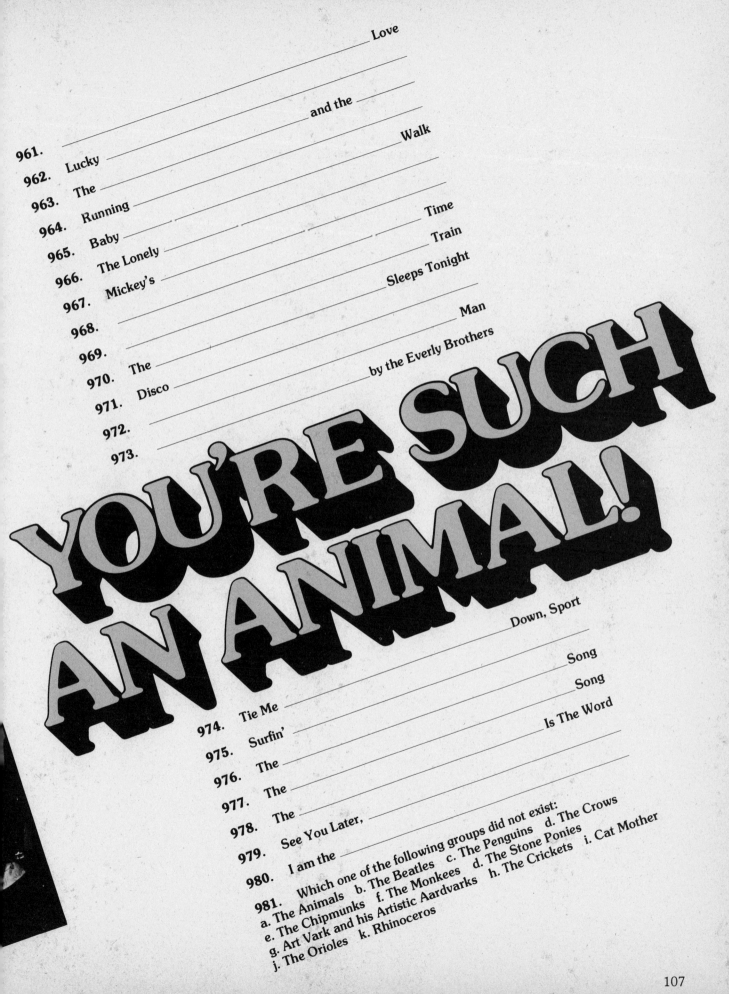

YOU'RE SUCH AN ANIMAL!

974. Tie Me _____ Down, Sport

975. Surfin' _____ Song

976. The _____ Song

977. The _____ Is The Word

978. The _____

979. See You Later, _____

980. I am the _____

981. Which one of the following groups did not exist:
a. The Animals   b. The Beatles   c. The Penguins   d. The Crows
e. The Chipmunks   f. The Monkees   g. The Stone Ponies
g. Art Vark and his Artistic Aardvarks   h. The Crickets   i. Cat Mother
j. The Orioles   k. Rhinoceros

${\cal P}$apa's Got a Brand New Mixed Bag!

Each correct answer in this grab bag of questions is worth one point.

982. Which of the following songs from the Broadway rock musical *Hair* was never made into a hit single? a. Aquarius b. Frank Mills c. Good Morning Starshine d. Let the Sun Shine In e. Hair f. Easy to be Hard

_____

_____

983. What motion picture did Simon and Garfunkel do the soundtrack for?

_____

_____

984. Name the group with which Janis Joplin had such hits as "Piece of My Heart" and "Ball and Chain."

_____

_____

985. In "Wake Up, Little Susie," the Everly Brothers promised to have her in by ten PM, but they fell asleep at a movie and didn't wake up until what time?

_____

_____

986. Which of the following songs by the Association tells about someone with "stormy eyes that flash at the sound of lies"? a. Along Comes Mary b. Cherish c. Never My Love d. Windy e. Requiem for the Masses

987. Which of the following singers was not killed in a 1959 plane crash? a. Richie Valens b. Buddy Holly c. The Big Bopper d. Don McLean

988. Which of the following Blood, Sweat and Tears songs featured Al Kooper as lead singer rather than David Clayton-Thomas or Steve Katz? a. And When I Die b. More Than You'll Ever Know c. Spinning Wheel d. Meagan's Gypsy Eyes e. You've Made Me So Very Happy

989. Match the song to the artist:

a. *School Days* ___Johnnie and Joe

b. *More Today Than Yesterday* ___We Five

c. *Morning Girl* ___Bruce Springsteen

d. *Come on Down to My Boat* ___Spiral Starecase

e. *You Were on My Mind* ___Chuck Berry

f. *Shake Your Booty* ___Every Mother's Son

g. *Over the Mountain, Across the Sea* ___Neon Philharmonic

h. *Born to Run* ___KC and the Sunshine Band

Fill in the correct month in each title:

990. _____ In the Rain by the Duprees

991. See You In _____ by the Tempos or the Happenings

992. _____ Love by Pat Boone

993. _____, _____, and _____ by Freddy Cannon

994. _____ Come She May by Simon and Garfunkel

995. First of _____ by the Bee Gees

996. Which of the following groups never had Eric Clapton as a member: a. The Yardbirds b. The Hollies c. Cream d. Blind Faith e. Derek and the Dominoes f. Delaney and Bonnie and Friends

997. Which of the following groups never had Ginger Baker as a drummer: a. Cream b. Blind Faith c. Baker's Dozen d. Ginger Baker's Air Force e. The Baker-Gurvitz Army

998. Lulu had one big American hit. It was the theme song to a motion picture. Was it: a. Blackboard Jungle b. Rock around the Clock c. Twist around the Clock d. Where the Boys Are e. The Happening f. To Sir with Love

Identify these stars after Clue A for 5 points, after Clue B for 3 points, and after Clue C for 1 point.

999. A. We were three members of the Champs, who recorded "Tequila" in 1958. B. Since then, one of us has had his own TV show and hits with "Gentle on My Mind" and "Rhinestone Cowboy." C. Two of us formed a singing duo and struck gold with songs like "Summer Breeze" and "Diamond Girl."

The three of us are?

1000. A. I began my career as a member of the Chad Mitchell Trio. B. I changed my name and wrote "Leaving on a Jet Plane" for Peter, Paul and Mary. C. After I hit the big time with "Take Me Home, Country Roads," all I could say was "Thank God I'm a Country Boy"!

My name is?

POINTS:

1001.

The Party's Over!

We've saved the toughest for last.
Before we sign off, we'll give you 10 points and a
chance to join Teen Angel in
that great Victrola in the sky if you can correctly
answer our last question:

How many grooves are there on a 45-rpm record
that has a three-minute song on one side and a
two-minute-twenty-nine second song on the other?

P O I N T S

Answers

Once Is Not Enough!

1.	b. Surfin' USA	7.	c. Rockin' Chair
2.	d. Kiss Me, Sailor	8.	b. Let's Twist Again
3.	a. Heartaches	9.	d. I've Got Sand in
4.	e. My Mammy		My Shoes
5.	a. The Same Old	10.	d. *Son of Schmilsson*
	Song	11.	c. Drift Away
6.	d. Judy's Turn to Cry	12.	e. Jo Ann Campbell

On the Street Where You Live!

13. The Beatles
14. The Orlons
15. The Drifters
16. The Fantastic Johnny C
17. Wilson Pickett
18. The Bee Gees
19. Tim Moore or Art Garfunkel
20. The Mamas and the Papas
21. The Nashville Teens
22. Lou Rawls
23. The Doors
24. Bob Dylan
25. The Beatles
26. Martha and the Vandellas
27. John Denver
28. The Beatles
29. Harper's Bizarre or Simon and Garfunkel

A Woman's Place Is in the Song!

30. Neil Diamond
31. Ray Charles
32. Gary Puckett and the Union Gap
33. Electric Light Orchestra
34. The Beatles
35. Crow
36. Santana
37. Stevie Wonder
38. Helen Reddy
39. Bob Dylan
40. Roy Orbison
41. Rolling Stones

Beatlemania!

42. George Harrison
43. Ringo Starr
44. Films: *A Hard Day's Night, Help!, Yellow Submarine, Let It Be;* TV Special: "Magical Mystery Tour;" Cartoon Series: *The Beatles*
45. *Live and Let Die*
46. Come and Get It
47. Badfinger
48. Cynthia
49. The ubiquitous Yoko Ono
50. "Well here's another clue for you all—The Walrus was Paul!"
51. Jane Asher
52. "The Inner Light" (flip-side to "Lady Madonna") and "You Know My Name" (flip-side to "Let It Be")
53. False. *Abbey Road* was an album of throwaways from the "Get Back" tapes, which later became the album *Let It Be.*

54. True. It was released as a single in 1966 and was later part of the album *Magical Mystery Tour.*
55. The soundtrack to *Yellow Submarine.*
56. I Want to Hold Your Hand
57. The Long and Winding Road
58. *Two Virgins*
59. The Ballad of John and Yoko
60. i.
61. The late Brian Epstein
62. George Martin. Phil Spector is credited with producing *Let It Be.*
63. Drummer Peter Best, who years later recorded an album entitled *Best of the Beatles.*
64. My Sweet Lord
65. Maharishi Mahesh Yogi
66. a.
67. *Sentimental Journey, Beaucoups of Blues, Ringo, Goodnight Vienna, A Blast from Your Past* (Greatest Hits), and *Ringo's Rotogravure*
68. *200 Motels*
69. f. (That was a toughie, wasn't it?)
70. Hey Jude
71. e. (Another toughie, huh?)
72. Tony Sheridan
73. The sitar
74. True. He died of a brain tumor.
75. Flying (on *Magical Mystery Tour*)
76. Bangladesh
77. e.
78. a. Played backwards, "Revolution No. 9" is a recording of a car crash and funeral, and John keeps saying "Turn me on, dead man."
    b. The front cover of *Abbey Road* was supposedly a funeral procession, the license plate on the Volkswagen said "28IF" and Paul would have been "28 if" he had lived, the back cover had some dots which, when connected, could read "3" Beatles.
    c. The hand over Paul's head on the cover of *Sgt. Pepper* was supposedly a death sign, they were standing over Paul's grave with his broken guitar next to it in a floral arrangement, Paul's back was to the viewer on the back cover which symbolized something or another, etc., etc.
    d. In the *Magical Mystery Tour* album Paul was the only one wearing a black carnation, a sign on his desk said "I was you" (referring to a double who supposedly had taken his place), the stars that made up the logo "Beatles" on the cover formed a phone number in London when you held them up to a mirror (supposedly if you called it on Wednesday morning at five o'clock, which is the day and time being pointed to on the back of "Sgt. Pepper," you would get the answer to the question "What happened to Paul?"), Paul was dressed as a black walrus, which supposedly meant something, too, etc., etc.
    e. John is apparently singing "I buried Paul" slowly at the end of the song.
79. *The Ed Sullivan Show*
80. *The Smothers Brothers Comedy Hour*
81. False. They only appeared on *Shindig.*
82. j.
83. "Don't Pass Me By" and "Octopus' Garden"
84. "Got to Get You into My Life" and "Ob-La-Di, Ob-La-Da"
85. Paul's dog

86. Shea Stadium
87. They were collarless.
88. In their ear. (Well, they do sing that "Penny Lane is in my ear," don't they?)
89. c. They were all Dave Clark Five hits.

The Leader of the Pack!

90. Buddy Holly and the Crickets
91. Martha Reeves and the Vandellas
92. Bob B. Soxx and the Blue Jeans
93. Gary Lewis and the Playboys
94. Little Anthony and the Imperials
95. Little Caesar and the Romans
96. Joey Dee and the Starliters
97. Archie Bell and the Drells
98. Maurice Williams and the Zodiacs
99. Tommy James and the Shondells
100. Duane Eddy and the Rebels
101. Junior Walker and the All-Stars
102. Huey "Piano" Smith and the Clowns
103. Eric Burdon and the Animals [also credit for War]
104. Cliff Richards and the Shadows
105. Bill Haley and the Comets
106. Sam the Sham and the Pharaohs
107. Kathy Young and the Innocents
108. Frankie Lymon and the Teenagers
109. Linda Ronstadt and the Stone Ponies
110. Mitch Ryder and the Detroit Wheels
111. Lee Andrews and the Hearts
112. Booker T. and the M.G.'s
113. Arlene Smith and the Chantels
114. Gary Puckett and the Union Gap
115. Hank Ballard and the Midnighters
116. Dickie Do and the Don'ts
117. Wayne Fontana and the Mindbenders
118. James Brown and the Famous Flames
119. B. Bumble and the Stingers
120. Gladys Knight and the Pips
121. Sonny Til and the Orioles
122. John Fred and the Playboy Band
123. Paul Revere and the Raiders
124. Desmond Dekker and the Aces
125. Patti LaBelle and the Blue-Bells
126. Patty Lace and the Petticoats
127. Billy J. Kramer and the Dakotas
128. Spanky and Our Gang
129. Sly and the Family Stone
130. Max Frost and the Troopers
131. Bo Donaldson and the Heywoods
132. Kenny Rogers and the First Edition

Number Please!

133.	Three	143.	Four	153.	Five
134.	Fifth	144.	Five	154.	Four
135.	Five	145.	First	155.	Five
136.	Five	146.	Four	156.	Four
137.	'66 or '77	147.	Fifth	157.	Ten
138.	IV	148.	Three	158.	Four
139.	Four Plus Two	149.	Four	159.	Three
140.	Five	150.	Five	160.	Four
141.	Four	151.	Six	161.	Ten
142.	Four	152.	Four	162.	Five

Dirty Songs!

163.	No	168.	No	173.	Yes
164.	No	169.	Yes	174.	No
165.	No	170.	No	175.	Yes
166.	Yes	171.	No	176.	No
167.	No	172.	No	177.	No

Monkee Business!

178. Last Train to Clarksville
179. Mickey Dolenz, then known as Mickey Braddock
180. Davy Jones
181. d. Head
182. Mike Nesmith
183. Peter Tork
184. Wool Hat
185. Drums
186. ColGems
187. Davy Jones, Mickey Dolenz, Tommy Boyce, and Bobby Hart

Food Glorious Food!

188. The Dartells
189. Dee Dee Sharp
190. Joey Dee and the Starliters
191. Dee Dee Sharp
192. Joey Dee and the Starliters
193. The Chordettes
194. Millie Small
195. The Four Seasons
196. George Hamilton IV
197. Lonnie Donegan
198. Jimmy Gilmer and the Fireballs
199. Booker T. and the M.G.'s
200. Herb Alpert and the Tijuana Brass
201. The Murmaids
202. Fats Domino
203. Tommy Roe
204. The Marathons
205. The Newbeats
206. Skip and Flip
207. Neil Diamond
208. Jay and the Techniques
209. Trini Lopez (or Peter, Paul and Mary)
210. The Pastel Six
211. John Lennon and the Plastic Ono Band
212. The Beatles

Yummy, Yummy, Chewy, Chewy, Fooie, Fooie!

213. Bobby Sherman
214. David Cassidy
215. Andy Kim
216. Love
217. Ron Dante
218. Don Kirshner
219. The 1910 Fruitgum Company
220. d.
221. d.
222. e.
223. c.

What's Your Name?

224.	Jean	259.	Bonnie
225.	Lucille	260.	Mary
226.	Sally	261.	Eleanor
227.	Molly	262.	Eleanor
228.	Fanny	263.	Rhonda
229.	Michelle	264.	Laura
230.	Peggy Sue	265.	Mary
231.	Susie	266.	Tammy
232.	Barbara Ann	267.	Mary Lou
233.	Sarah	268.	Sally
234.	Judy	269.	Denise
235.	Judy	270.	Judy
236.	Lucy	271.	Cindy Oh Cindy
237.	Paula	272.	Lucretia
238.	Carrie Ann	273.	Ruby
239.	Holly	274.	Ruby
240.	Linda	275.	Diana
241.	Lulu	276.	Dinah
242.	Sheila	277.	Gloria
243.	Hazel	278.	Maybelline
244.	Susan	279.	Nadine
245.	Alice	280.	Annie
246.	Sherry	281.	Cathy
247.	Dawn	282.	Sue
248.	Ronnie	283.	Dolly
249.	Connie	284.	Mary
250.	Marianne	285.	Jennifer
251.	Carol	286.	Juliet
252.	Sue	287.	Delilah
253.	Donna	288.	Candy
254.	Donna	289.	Valerie
255.	Julie	290.	Jane
256.	Rose	291.	Bernadette
257.	Mona Lisa	292.	Caroline
258.	Abigail		

Mish-Mosh!

293. e.   294. a.   295. f.   296. a.   297. f.

298. Stevie Wonder/*Tamla*
Chuck Berry/*Chess*
Little Richard/*Specialty*
The Platters/*Mercury*
Chubby Checker/*Parkway*

299. a.   300. d.   301. c.

302. False. He is a fictional character whose voice was supplied by Ross Bagdasarian.

303. b.

304. Oh Happy Day/*The Edwin Hawkins Singers*
Oh How Happy/*Shades of Blue*
Happy Days/*Pratt and McClain*
Happy Birthday Sweet Sixteen/*Neil Sedaka*
Happy, Happy Birthday Baby/*The Tune Weavers*
The Happy Organ/*Dave "Baby" Cortez*
If You Wanna Be Happy/*Jimmy Soul*
Happy Together/*The Turtles*

305. a.   306. c.   307. a.   308. b.

Elvis Pelvis!

309. c. Colonel Parker
310. b. *The Ed Sullivan Show*

311. A man on a fuzzy tree
312. a. Whole Lotta Shakin' Goin' On
313. "Well, you ain't never caught a rabbit!"
314. Don't Be Cruel
315. d. The Jordanaires
316. Lonely Street
317. It's Now or Never
318. d. Love Me Tender
319. c. Graceland
320. a. Ghetto   b. Want, Need, Love   c. Devil
      d. Chapel   e. Jailhouse

Mr., Mrs. and Miss!

321.	Mr.	331.	Mrs.
322.	Mrs.	332.	Mr.
323.	Miss	333.	Mr.
324.	Mr.	334.	Mr.
325.	Mr.	335.	Mr.
326.	Mr.	336.	Mr.
327.	Mrs.	337.	Mr.
328.	Mr.	338.	Mr.
329.	Mr.	339.	Mr.
330.	Mr.	340.	Mr.

Do You Wanna Dance?

341.	The Capitols	352.	Freddie and the Dreamers
342.	The Orlons	353.	Soupy Sales
343.	The Dovells	354.	Eydie Gormé
344.	Bobby Freeman or the Butterflys	355.	Major Lance
345.	The Olympics	356.	Little Eva
346.	Joey Dee and the Starliters	357.	The Larks
347.	Chubby Checker	358.	The Vibrations
348.	Chubby Checker	359.	Chubby Checker
349.	Chubby Checker	360.	Van McCoy
350.	Dee Dee Sharp		
351.	The Diamonds		

Clothes Call!

361. A White Sport Coat and a Pink Carnation/*Marty Robbins*
Tan Shoes with Pink Shoe Laces/*Dodie Stevens*
Blue Suede Shoes/*Carl Perkins*
Bobbie Socks to Stockings/*Frankie Avalon*
Venus in Blue Jeans/*Jimmy Clanton*
Black Denim Trousers/*The Cheers*
These Boots Are Made for Walking/*Nancy Sinatra*
Chantilly Lace/*The Big Bopper*
Lipstick on Your Collar/*Connie Francis*
Penny Loafers and Bobby Sox/*Joe Bennett and the Sparkletones*
Sand in My Shoes/*The Drifters*
Short Shorts/*The Royal Teens*
Itsy Bitsy Teeny Weeny Yellow Polka Dot Bikini/*Brian Hyland*

Heart and Soul!

362. They've abandoned the Motor City for Tinseltown—Los Angeles.
363. True
364. I Heard It Through the Grapevine
365. e. Dinah Shore

366. False
367. Fingertips Part Two
368. Harmonica
369. Twelve years old
370. Martha and the Vandellas (Is a vandella a lady vandal?)
371. The Marvelettes (Must be a female marvel!)
372. The Temptations (Male Temptationettes?)
373. Stevie Wonder
374. Mary Wells
375. William "Smokey" Robinson
376. The Jackson Five
377. d. MoMoney
378. Steve Wonder—just read it backward!
379. The Miracles
380. Barrett Strong
381. The Contours

The Grateful Dead!

382. "Teen Angel" by Mark Dinning
383. "Laurie (Strange Things Happen in This World)" by Dickey Lee
384. "Tell Laura I Love Her" by Ray Peterson
385. "Last Kiss" by J. Frank Wilson and the Cavaliers
386. "Leader of the Pack" by the Shangri-Las
387. "Leader of the Laundromat" by the Detergents
388. "Honey" by Bobby Goldsboro
389. "Dead Man's Curve" by Jan and Dean

Hometown Honeys!

390. Dion and the Belmonts/*Bronx, New York*
Gerry and the Pacemakers/*Liverpool, England*
Jefferson Airplane/*San Francisco, California*
Bobby Rydell/*Philadelphia, Pennsylvania*
The Buckinghams/*Chicago, Illinois*
KC and the Sunshine Band/*Jacksonville, Florida*
Paul Anka/*Toronto, Canada*
The Rolling Stones/*London, England*
The Doors/*Los Angeles, California*
Kool and the Gang/*Jersey City, New Jersey*
Little Richard/*Macon, Georgia*
Abba/*Sweden*
The Kingsmen/*Portland, Oregon*
The Supremes/*Detroit, Michigan*
Bob Dylan/*Hibbings, Minnesota*
Helen Reddy/*Australia*
Chuck Berry/*St. Louis, Missouri*
Bob Marley and the Wailers/*Kingston, Jamaica*
Orpheus/*Boston, Massachusetts*
Elvis Presley/*Memphis, Tennessee*

The Great American Novelty Song!

391. Leader of the Pack
392. Mother-in-Law
393. Carole King's answer to Neil Sedaka's "Oh, Carol"
394. Duke of Earl
395. Big Bad John
396. Mrs. Brown, You've Got a Lovely Daughter
397. King of the Road
398. Battle of New Orleans
399. A Boy Named Sue

The Royalty of Rock!

400.	King	405.	King, King
401.	Queen	406.	Sir
402.	King	407.	King
403.	Duke	408.	King
404.	King	409.	King

Crazy Titles!

410. The Chords or The Crewcuts
411. The Diamonds
412. Bob B. Soxx and the Blue Jeans
413. Manfred Mann or The Shirelles
414. Little Anthony and the Imperials
415. Major Lance
416. Steam
417. Dickie Do and the Don'ts
418. The Playmates
419. The Edsels
420. Chuck Berry
421. The Crystals or Ian Matthews or Shaun Cassidy
422. The Hollywood Argyles
423. The Delfonics
424. Lee Dorsey
425. The Archies
426. Harry Belafonte
427. The Rivingtons
428. The Beatles
429. Manfred Mann
430. Daddy Dewdrop
431. Johnny Thunder
432. LaVern Baker

T for Two!

433.
a. Gene McDaniels
b. Bobby Lewis
c. The Exciters
d. Bobby Vee
e. The Crests
f. Natalie Cole
g. The Mello-Kings
h. Fabian
i. The Byrds
j. The Cyrkle
k. The Classics IV
l. The Zombies
m. The Chambers Brothers
n. Little Anthony and the Imperials
o. Johnny Rivers
p. The Fleetwoods
q. The Five Satins
r. Three Dog Night
s. Lou Christie
t. Bachman-Turner Overdrive

Dynamic Duos!

434.
a.	Jeremy	i.	Dave
b.	Gordon	j.	Juan
c.	Sylvia	k.	Joe
d.	Sylvia	l.	April Stevens
e.	Lee	m.	Dee Dee
f.	Lilly	n.	Paula
g.	Garfunkel	o.	Cher
h.	Dean	p.	Crofts

The Supreme Sacrifice!

435. Motown
436. Where Did Our Love Go?, Baby Love, Come See About Me, Stop! In the Name of Love, Back in My Arms Again, I Hear a Symphony
437. Cindy Birdsong
438. Jean Terrell
439. Someday We'll Be Together
440. Go Up the Ladder to the Roof
441. Holland, Dozier and Holland
442. The Happening
443. I'm Gonna Make You Love Me
444. *Lady Sings the Blues, Mahogany, The Wiz*

Songs That Were Instrumental to Rock 'n' Roll!

445.	Yes	454.	No	463.	No
446.	No	455.	Yes	464.	Yes
447.	Yes	456.	Yes	465.	No
448.	No	457.	No	466.	No
449.	Yes	458.	Yes	467.	Yes
450.	No	459.	Yes	468.	Yes
451.	Yes	460.	Yes	469.	No
452.	Yes	461.	No		
453.	Yes	462.	Yes		

Elton!

470. Reginald Kenneth Dwight
471. c. Bluesology
472. Elton came from saxophonist Elton Dean and John came from Bluesology leader Long John Baldry. No, he was not inspired by Olivia Newton-John!
473. The Pinball Wizard
474. Kiki Dee
475. Neil Sedaka
476. The Rocket Record Company
477. Piano
478. Bernie Taupin
479. c. by mail
480. e. Elton John
481. *Friends* (Who could ever forget?)
482. Lucy in the Sky with Diamonds
483. Sorry Seems to Be the Hardest Word (For some of us, octodecillionth is the hardest word, but who's to quibble with Elton?)
484. d. Watford Hornets Soccer Club
485. Billie Jean King—then playing with the soon-to-be-defunct Philadelphia Freedoms of World Team Tennis.
486. c. Marilyn Monroe (Why is it that no one ever writes a song about Porky Pig?)
487. We like to think of Elton as married to his music.
488. d. Two hundred pairs—to the undying gratitude of optometrists everywhere.
489. e. The Yellow Brick Road

Color My World!

490.	Golden	496.	Red/Blue
491.	Blue/Blue (or White/White)	497.	Black
		498.	White/Pink
492.	Purple	499.	Blue
493.	Tan/Pink	500.	Blue
494.	Blue	501.	Brown
495.	Yellow	502.	Red

503.	Brown	517.	Red
504.	Black	518.	Yellow
505.	Blue	519.	Blue
506.	Black	520.	White
507.	Blues	521.	Black/Black
508.	Green	522.	Red
509.	Blue	523.	Yellow
510.	Blue	524.	Purple
511.	Blue	525.	Crimson
512.	Blue	526.	Green
513.	Green	527.	Gold
514.	Yellow	528.	Green
515.	White	529.	Brown/Blue
516.	Red		

Only the Names Have Been Changed to Protect the Innocent!

530.
a. Richard Starkey
b. Robert Zimmerman
c. Steveland Morris
d. Ernest Evans
e. J. P. Richardson
f. Charlie Westover
g. Marsha Blanc
h. Richard Penniman
i. Robert Waldon Cassatto
j. Peter Noone
k. Ellas McDaniels
l. Carol Klein
m. Ross Bagdasarian

College of Musical Knowledge!

531. Soldier Boy
532. Sweet Loretta Martin thought she was a woman, but she was another man—in the Beatles' song "Get Back." (She is also the wife of Beatles producer George Martin.)
533. Desmond and Molly Jones
534. Rory Storm and the Hurricanes
535. On Blueberry Hill
536. Rubber Duck, good buddy
537.
a. The Shocking Blue
b. Blue Suede
c. Harold Melvin and the Bluenotes
d. Blue Oyster Cult
538. True—they were then known as the Hawks
539. Short People
540. Because it wouldn't be right to leave your best girl home on a Saturday night!
541. What else? Dusk
542. Twelfth Street and Vine
543. False
544. d. Tom and Jerry

Family Affair!

545.	Mama	552.	Cousins
546.	Daddy	553.	Dad
547.	Brother	554.	Papa
548.	Mother	555.	Son
549.	Ma	556.	Daddy
550.	Papa	557.	Muddah, Faddah
551.	Mama	558.	Daddy

The Guess Who!

559.	James Taylor	564.	Roger Miller
560.	Jim Croce	565.	Barry Manilow
561.	John Sebastian	566.	Ray Charles
562.	Neil Sedaka	567.	Chuck Berry
563.	Frankie Avalon	568.	Mama Cass Elliott

Re-Recorded!

569. Gladys Knight and the Pips, Marvin Gaye, and Creedence Clearwater Revival
570. Little Eva and Grand Funk Railroad
571. Bobby Freeman, the Beach Boys, the Mamas and the Papas, and Bette Midler
572. The Contours and the Dave Clark Five
573. Eddie Cochran, Blue Cheer, and the Who
574. Chuck Berry, the Beach Boys, and the Beatles
575. The Four Seasons and the Tremeloes
576. Sam Cooke and Cat Stevens
577. Creedence Clearwater Revival and Ike and Tina Turner
578. Ben E. King, Spider Turner, and John Lennon
579. Dusty Springfield and the Bay City Rollers
580. The Beatles and Anne Murray
581. Harold Dorman and Johnny Rivers
582. The Platters and Ringo Starr
583. The Everly Brothers and Linda Ronstadt
584. The Isley Brothers and Joey Dee and the Starliters
585. Sam Cooke and Herman's Hermits
586. Dale Hawkins and Creedence Clearwater Revival
587. The Doors and José Feliciano

Take Me to Your Leader!

588. John Sebastian
589. Fred Parris
590. David Gates
591. Ronnie Spector
592. Van Morrison
593. Roger Daltrey
594. Burton Cummings, Jr.
595. Todd Rundgren
596. Johnny Maestro
597. John Fogerty
598. Smokey Robinson
599. Stevie Winwood
600. Dennis Yost
601. Eric Carmen

602. Jim Morrison
603. Levi Stubbs
604. Harvey Fuqua
605. Roger McGuinn
606. Tony Williams
607. Jimmy Beaumont
608. Paul Rodgers
609. Jay Black
610. Michael Jackson

The People's Choice!

611. a. The Gentrys
612. c. The Safaris
613. e. Barry and the Tamerlanes (Later, Boyce and Hart had a hit with a different song and the same title!)
614. d. The Spencer Davis Group
615. c. The Dell-Vikings
616. d. The Foundations
617. b. Connie Francis
618. c. Gene Pitney
619. d. The Elegants

What Kind of Fool Am I?

620. Fools Rush In/*Brook Benton*
Poor Little Fool/*Ricky Nelson*
Everybody's Somebody's Fool/*Connie Francis*
Fool on the Hill/*The Beatles*
Foolish Little Girl/*The Shirelles*
What Kind of Fool Do You Think I Am?/*The Tams*
What Kind of Fool Am I?/*Sammy Davis, Jr.*
Why Do Fools Fall in Love?/*Frankie Lymon and the Teenagers*

The Name Game!

621.	Michael	640.	Freddie	659.	Mickey
622.	Norman	641.	Earl	660.	Joe
623.	John	642.	Louie, Louie	661.	Leroy
624.	Bobby	643.	Joe	662.	Johnny
625.	Bobby	644.	Tommy	663.	Harry
626.	Johnny	645.	Mickey	664.	Ahab
627.	Henry	646.	Julio	665.	Joe
628.	Johnny	647.	Pepino	666.	Alfie
629.	Rudolph	648.	Joe	667.	Billy
630.	Alvin	649.	Mack	668.	Tom
631.	Eddie	650.	Louie	669.	Edmund
632.	Michael	651.	Charlie	670.	Timothy
633.	Rocky	652.	Paul	671.	Billy
634.	Bill	653.	Jim	672.	Jude
635.	Billy Joe	654.	Bill	673.	John
636.	Larry	655.	Lee	674.	Bennie
637.	Jack	656.	Davy	675.	Henry
638.	Fernando	657.	Johnny		
639.	John	658.	Peter		

Every Cloud Has a Silver Lining . . . or a Gold Record!

676.
  a. The Beatles
  b. Dee Clark
  c. The Dramatics
  d. Neil Sedaka
  e. The Ronettes
  f. Love Unlimited
  g. Lou Christie
  h. The Cascades
  i. The Cowsills
  j. The Lovin' Spoonful
  k. Creedence Clearwater Revival
  l. B. J. Thomas
  m. Glenn Yarborough
  n. The Temptations
  o. Buddy Holly
  p. Creedence Clearwater Revival
  q. The Guess Who
  r. Brook Benton
  s. Bob Dylan
  t. Davy Jones
  u. The Fortunes
  v. James Taylor
  w. The Critters

The Gang's All Here!

677. Cass Elliot, Denny Dougherty, John Phillips, Michelle Gilliam Phillips
678. Eddie Brigati, Felix Cavaliere, Gene Cornish, Dino Danelli
679. Roger Daltrey, Keith Moon, Peter Townshend, John Entwistle
680. Alvin, Theodore, Simon, and David Seville
681. Mike Love, Brian Wilson, Carl Wilson, Dennis Wilson, Al Jardine
682. Jim Morrison, Ray Manzarak, Robbie Krieger, John Densmore
683. Cory Wells, Danny Hutton, Chuck Negron
684. Eric Clapton, Jack Bruce, Ginger Baker
685. Mick Fleetwood, Stevie Nicks, Lindsey Buckingham, John McVie, Christine Perfect McVie
686. Barry, Maurice, and Robin Gibb

687. Mick Jagger, Keith Richards, Bill Wyman, Charlie Watts, Brian Jones
688. Bobby Hatfield and Bill Medley
689. Eric Clapton, Ginger Baker, Steve Winwood, Rich Grech
690. Frankie Valli, Bob Gaudio, Nick Massi, Tommy DaVito
691. Davy Jones, Mike Nesmith, Peter Tork, Mickey Dolenz
692. Tim Hauser, Janis Segal, Alan Paul, Laurel Masse

Executive Suite!

693. Lou Adler/*Ode*
    Herb Alpert/*A&M*
    Neil Bogart/*Casablanca*
    Clive Davis/*Arista*
    Ahmet Ertegun/*Atlantic*
    David Geffen/*Asylum*
    Berry Gordy/*Motown*
    Florence Greenberg/*Scepter*
    Sam Phillips/*Sun*
    Phil Spector/*Phillies*

Potpourri for the Expert!

694. f. Disco Duck
695. d. Ken "Eddie Haskell" Osmond (No fans—he really isn't Alice Cooper. And he sure isn't one of the Osmond Brothers!)
696. j. The Fugitive
697. a. The Jefferson Airplane b. Queen c. The Bee Gees d. The Shirelles e. Rod Stewart
698. a. Friday b. Tuesday c. Sunday d. Saturday e. Monday, Monday
699. The Chicago Transit Authority
700. d. I Started a Fire
701. c. Crop of the Cream, and f. Cream, Cheese, and Bagels

Sons of the Beach!

702. North—the way they kiss; South—the way they talk; East—they're hip—the Beach Boys dig the styles they wear; and Midwest—they make you feel all right!
703. Sweet Little Sixteen
704. g. Al Jolson—but think what a terrific Beach Boy he would have made!
705. The father of Brian, Carl, and Dennis, the Beach Boys' early manager, and the head of their publishing company.
706. Brothers Records
707. f. I Sunburned My Armpits on Redondo Beach
708. "Till her daddy takes her T-Bird away."
709. *Pet Sounds*
710. *Smiley Smile*
711. Little Honda
712. The Hondells (Who else?)
713. Rhonda
714. *Holland*
715. Yep—Jan Berry and Dean Torrence
716. Mitch Ryder—who later found fame in the Detroit smog
717. The Surfaris
718. Little GTO—Ronnie and the Daytonas; Little Deuce Coupe—the Beach Boys; Drag City—Jan and Dean; Hey Little Cobra—the Ripchords; Walk, Don't Run—the Ventures

I'm a Travelin' Man!

719. Neil Diamond
720. Elvis Presley
721. The Ventures
722. Johnny Horton
723. R. Dean Taylor
724. Mark Lindsay
725. Mitch Miller
726. Crosby, Stills, Nash and Young
727. The Bee Gees
728. Lynyrd Skynyrd
729. Boz Scaggs
730. Ray Charles
731. Gladys Knight and the Pips
732. Brook Benton
733. Vickie Lawrence
734. The Mamas and the Papas
735. Lesley Gore
736. The Rivieras
737. The Beach Boys
738. Simon and Garfunkel
739. The Ritchie Family
740. Roger Miller
741. The Coasters
742. The Beatles
743. The Steve Miller Band

Body Language!

744. Finger
745. Arms
746. Hand
747. Head
748. Eyes
749. Neck
750. Heart
751. Hair
752. Hand, Hand
753. Skin
754. Head, Shoulder
755. Heart
756. Eyes
757. Heart
758. Back (Ugh!)

Croon the Tune, Then Place the Face!

759. Ray Charles
760. Tommy James and the Shondells
761. Petula Clark
762. Sam Cooke
763. Fats Domino
764. Bobby Darin
765. The Everly Brothers
766. The Young Rascals
767. The Rolling Stones
768. Neil Diamond
769. Bob Dylan
770. Simon and Garfunkel
771. Eagles
772. Donovan
773. Chicago

The Guess Who—Part Two!

774. Ben E. King
775. Stephen Stills
776. Bill Haley and the Comets
777. Rod Stewart
778. Leon Russell

Number Please!

779.	9	797.	Twenty-six
780.	Million, One	798.	Twenty-five
781.	Sixteen	799.	Thousand
782.	Sixteen	800.	VIII
783.	Fifty	801.	Ten
784.	A Thousand	802.	Twenty-five or six to four
785.	Ninety-six	803.	Seventeen
786.	Three	804.	A Thousand
787.	One	805.	Seven
788.	66	806.	Sixty-seven and Sixty-eight
789.	Five	807.	Three
790.	Three	808.	One, Two, Three
791.	Sixteen	809.	One
792.	Million	810.	Nine
793.	Nineteenth	811.	Seven
794.	4–5789	812.	A Thousand
795.	A Hundred	813.	One
796.	Sixteen		

Devil or Angel!

814. d. Bobby Vee *and* b. The Clovers
815. c. Elvis Presley
816. b. Mitch Ryder and the Detroit Wheels
817. a. Cliff Richards
818. e. The Rolling Stones
819. c. Merilee Rush
820. b. The Penguins
821. a. Shelley Fabares
822. e. Neil Sedaka
823. b. The Crests
824. c. The Vogues
825. c. Curtis Lee
826. a. Mark Dinning
827. d. Roy Orbison
828. e. The Captain and Tennille

Know Your Basic Food Groups!

829. The Raspberries
830. The Lemon Pipers
831. Hot Chocolate
832. Vanilla Fudge
833. Peaches and Herb
834. Soupy Sales (Whew!!!)
835. The Strawberry Alarm Clock
836. The Peppermint Rainbow
837. The Cookies
838. Shep and the Limelites

It's Only Words!

839. The 3rd of June
840. millionaire, president
841. Santa Catalina
842. e. Chuck
843. Does Your Chewing Gum Lose Its Flavor on the Bedpost Overnight?
844. Hope
845. a. Joe Spivey
     b. Leonard Skinner
     c. Jeffrey Hardy
     d. Aunt Bertha

846. fifty cents
847. "We'll be right in seventh heaven!"
848. Jack, Stan, Roy, Gus, and Lee
849. 1) You love her with all your heart.
     2) You tell her you're never ever going to part.
     3) Remember the meaning of romance.
     4) You break up, but you give her just one more chance.
850. Goodnight, Sweetheart, Goodnight (by the Spaniels)
851. on Thirty-fourth and Vine
852. It smelled like turpentine. It looked like India ink.
853. Palisades Park. Chuck Barris, of *Gong Show* fame, wrote it.

A Near Ms.!

854. a. The Crystals
     b. The Ronettes
     c. The Shangri-Las
     d. The Angels
     e. The Chiffons
     f. Reparata and the Delrons
     g. Rosie and the Originals
     h. The Chantels
     i. The Shirelles
     j. The Charmettes
     k. The Chordettes
     l. The Bobbettes
     m. The Jaynettes
     n. Merci
     o. The Poni-Tails

They're Really Rockin' in Boston, Pittsburgh, Pa.!

855. Dave Loggins
856. The Ad Libs
857. The Excellents
858. Ben E. King
859. Bobby Rydell
860. The Elton John Band
861. MFSB
862. The Association
863. Bobby Bare
864. Paper Lace
865. The Lovin' Spoonful
866. Chuck Berry [also Lonnie Mack and Johnny Rivers]
867. Freddy Cannon
868. Gary "U.S." Bonds
869. Arlo Guthrie
870. Fats Domino
871. Johnny Horton
872. Freddy Cannon
873. Wilbert Harrison
874. Glen Campbell
875. Marty Robbins
876. Glen Campbell
877. The Doors
878. Kool and the Gang
879. Jan and Dean
880. Dionne Warwick
881. Scott McKenzie
882. Eric Burdon and the Animals
883. Perry Como
884. Jan and Dean

Woodstock!

885.	Yes	895.	Yes	905.	No
886.	Yes	896.	No	906.	Yes
887.	No	897.	No	907.	Yes
888.	Yes	898.	Yes	908.	No
889.	Yes	899.	Yes	909.	Yes
890.	No	900.	No	910.	No
891.	No	901.	Yes	911.	No
892.	Yes	902.	Yes	912.	Yes
893.	Yes	903.	No	913.	No
894.	Yes	904.	Yes		

The British Are Coming!

914. Needles and Pins
915. d. Love Potion No. 9
916. Ferry Cross the Mersey
917. b. The Yardbirds
918. d. Freddie and the Dreamers
919. "No Milk Today"
920. Satisfaction
921. The Hollies
922. a. She's Not There
    b. Whole Lotta Love
    c. Pinball Wizard
    d. I'm Crying
    e. Little Children
923. c. Uncle Ernie
924. See Me, Feel Me, Touch Me, Heal Me (c, d, a, and b)
925. Sha La La
926. The House of the Rising Sun
927. We Gotta Get Out of This Place
928. In a "World Without Love"
929. The Dave Clark Five
930. c. Go Now
931. Eight! Seven times before plus Henry.
932. In Memphis
933. True—they hailed from London, not Nashville!

Do You Believe in Magic?

934. This Magic Moment/The Drifters/Jay and the Americans
935. Magic Carpet Ride/Steppenwolf
936. Magic Man/Heart
937. Black Magic Woman/Santana
938. That Old Black Magic/Bobby Darin
939. Magical Mystery Tour/The Beatles
940. It's Magic/Pilot
941. Puff the Magic Dragon/Peter, Paul and Mary
942. Strange Magic/Electric Light Orchestra
943. My Baby Must Be a Magician/Marvelettes
944. Could This Be Magic?/The Dubs
945. Could It Be Magic?/Barry Manilow
946. Do You Believe in Magic?/The Lovin' Spoonful
947. You Made Me Believe in Magic/The Bay City Rollers

Boys and Girls Together!

948.	boys and girls	954.	boys
949.	boys	955.	boys and girls
950.	boys and girls	956.	girls
951.	girls	957.	boys
952.	boys and girls	958.	boys and girls
953.	boys	959.	boys and girls

March of the Horribles!

960. a. Bubi and Bob
    b. Buchanan and Ancell
    c. The Five Blobs
    d. David Seville
    e. The Randells
    f. Zacherle
    g. The Frantics
    h. Randy Fuller
    i. Bobby "Boris" Pickett
    j. Fats Domino
    k. Gene and Wendell
    l. Jumpin' Gene Simmons
    m. Phil Harris
    n. Nervous Norvus
    o. Sheb Wooley

You're Such an Animal!

961.	Puppy	972.	Hound Dog
962.	Ladybug	973.	Bird Dog
963.	Birds, Bees	974.	Kangaroo
964.	Bear	975.	Bird
965.	Elephant	976.	Boll Weevil
966.	Bull	977.	Chipmunk
967.	Monkey	978.	Bird
968.	Monkey or Pony	979.	Alligator
969.	Mule	980.	Walrus
970.	Lion	981.	g. Art Vark and his Artistic Aardvarks (Surprised?)
971.	Duck		

Papa's Got a Brand New Mixed Bag!

982. b. Frank Mills
983. *The Graduate*
984. Big Brother and the Holding Company
985. Four o'clock
986. d. Windy
987. d. Don McLean
988. b. More Than You'll Ever Know
989. a. Chuck Berry
    b. Spiral Starecase
    c. Neon Philharmonic
    d. Every Mother's Son
    e. We Five
    f. KC and the Sunshine Band
    g. Johnnie and Joe
    h. Bruce Springsteen
990. September
991. September
992. April
993. June, July, and August
994. April
995. May
996. b. The Hollies
997. c. Baker's Dozen
998. f. To Sir with Love
999. Glen Campbell and Seals and Crofts
1000. John Denver

The Party's Over!

1001. There are two grooves on any normal 45 RPM record—one groove to each side!

Rate-a-Record!

Add up the number of points you received for answering our questions correctly. Now rate yourself. Give yourself an extra point if you've got a good beat but you can't dance to it.

If you scored a total of **1,400** to **1,455** you are "The Leader of the Pack"—put on your 1950's official Arthur Fonzarelli black leather jacket, because you're the coolest when it comes to answering rock 'n' roll trivia questions.

A score of **1,310** to **1,399** means "(Baby) You Got What It Takes"—to score so high that it qualifies you as runner-up to the "Leader of the Pack." If for any reason the Leader of the Pack cannot fulfill his trivia king duties in the coming year, you will assume the title.

A score of **1,165** to **1,309** makes you a "Teen Angel"— the "Soul and Inspiration" to rock 'n' roll trivia players around the world. You rocked this test and rolled up an impressive score.

A score of **1,020** to **1,164** should bring you "Satisfaction." You no longer have to sing, "I can't get no!"

If you scored **950** to **1,019** you've done fairly well. Just remember that in the world of rock 'n' roll trivia "You Don't Have to Be a Star (Baby)."

A score of **875** to **950** brings to mind the wise saying "Don't Think Twice." You didn't about too many questions.

A score of **800** to **874** should prompt you to scream the title of an old Beach Boys tune—"HELP ME, RHONDA"!

If you scored **730** to **799** you should be singing with the Beatles—"I Should've Known Better."

If you scored **660** to **729** and refuse to accept any fault, "Blame It on the Bossa Nova."

A score of **585** to **659** gives you the rock 'n' roll trivia title as "The Great Pretender."

If you scored **440** to **584**, welcome to the rank of "Nowhere Man."

If you scored **296** to **439** you may as well "Hit the Road, Jack."

A score of **150** to **295** should remind you of the old Beatles tune, "I'm a Loser."

As to anyone who scored less than **150**, "God Only Knows!"

Every Picture Tells a Story!

For those of you who looked at the faces of the rock 'n' roll stars in this book and figured they couldn't all be the Who, the Guess Who, the Wonder Who or Question Mark and the Mysterians, we have provided this handy answer key.

Pages 6 and 7 (top, left and right): the Mamas and the Papas and the Bee Gees. Bottom row, left to right: the Band, the Beatles the way your parents would have preferred them in 1964, and Elvis.

Pages 8 and 9 (top to bottom): the Rolling Stones, Chubby Checker, and Wings.

Page 15, top: Chicago. Bottom, the "Godfather of Soul"—James Brown.

Pages 16 and 17 (top, left to right): Neil Diamond, Bill Haley and the Comets, Bob Dylan, the Miracles (post-Smokey Robinson era), and Tom Jones. Bottom row, left to right: the Jackson Five, Carole King, Kenny Rogers, and the tartan-clad Bay City Rollers.

Pages 28–33: Those lovable moptops, that fab foursome—the Beatles! In case you've forgotten, they are, from left to right on pages 28 and 29: Paul, Ringo, George and John. (Photo on pages 28 and 29, individual portraits on page 31, and large photo on page 33 from Nempix.)

Pages 38 and 39 (top row, left to right): David Bowie, Connie Francis, the Jefferson Starship, and Darryl Hall (without John Oates). Second row, left to right: the Duprees and the Who. Bottom row, left to right: Manhattan Transfer, James Taylor, and Harold Melvin and the Bluenotes.

Pages 50 and 51 (top row, left to right): the Four Tops, Harry Nilsson, and Fleetwood Mac. Second row, left to right: the Everly Brothers, the Moonglows, and Chuck Berry, and disco queen Gloria Gaynor. Bottom row, left to right: Natalie Cole, Rhymin' Paul Simon, the Animals, and the Jesters.

Pages 68 and 69 (top row, left to right): Supersinger Barbra Streisand, Peter, Paul and Mary, Steve Miller, Ray Charles, and the Four Seasons (all five of them). Second row, left to right: Crosby, Stills and Nash, Roger Daltrey (of the Who), Maxine Nightingale, and the Duprees. Bottom row, left to right: the Isley Brothers, and Barry Manilow (photo by Lee Gurst).

Pages 82 and 83 (top row, left to right): "Lady Soul"—Aretha Franklin, John Denver, Rod Stewart, Boz Scaggs (a great name in rock 'n' roll). Row two, left to right: the Beach Boys, Donovan and his band, and Ben E. King. Bottom row, left to right: Olivia Newton-John, Cat Stevens, and the Tremeloes.

Pages 98 and 99 (top, left to right): The Supremes, Patti Smith (photo by Judy Linn), Sly Stewart (without the Family Stone), Bette Midler on the half shell, and Rita Coolidge. Row two, left to right: ABBA, Mary and Leon Russell. Bottom, left to right: Linda and Paul McCartney, Peter, Paul and Mary, Rick Nelson, and Led Zeppelin.

Back Cover: Natalie Cole, the Beatles, and those all-new, all-now, all-American disc jockeys and authors—Broadway Bruce Solomon and Madcap Michael Uslan! (Authors' photo by Adrienne Morea.)
Cover photographs painted by Wendy Frost.

Cousins Brucie and Michael wish to thank the very talented Joe Szabo for allowing us to reproduce some of his amazing photographs of teenagers and their life-styles. Harmony Books is publishing Joe's new book of photographs entitled *Almost Grown,* which we strongly recommend.

There are three people whose talents, skills, and enthusiasm are directly responsible for making this book possible and making it good: agent and friend extraordinaire, Susie Breitner (apparently the same Susie that the Everly Brothers, Dale Hawkins, the Buckinghams, Dion, Creedence, and the Mothers immortalized in song); Linda Sunshine, ace editor and beneficent overlord, whose work has led us to call her "Sunshine Superman" (if she ever knocks on your door, we suggest you "Let the Sunshine In"); Barbara Jackson, the person who kept the book (and us) together during all this and worked so hard you'd swear you had the Jackson *Five* working all at once! Special gratitude to art director Judy Lee and designer Joel Avirom for making the words and pictures really sing.

Finally, our thanks and appreciation to everyone else who made this volume possible, particularly, Al Fernandez of A. Devaney & Co. for their 1950's pictures; Pauline Finkelstein of Simon and Schuster; Vogel's Record Shop in Elizabeth, New Jersey; Irene Vargas and Rachel Tedesco, UA's supertypists; Libby Mark, who went to school at U. of W. and never met Bruce; Leah Cohen, former cheerleader and picture supplier; Paul Uslan, for all his 45's; Paul Hyman, for sharing his knowledge; Glen Solomon, for knowing more than anyone; Larry Friedman of UA Records; Loren Chardez of Columbia Records; Caroline Prutzman of ABC Records; Maureen O'Connor of Capitol Records; Bob Seidenberg of Warner Communications; Harry Mielke; Candy Schwefel for the prom picture; Mary Jo Myszelow of RCA Records; Melanie Rogers of Arista Records; Lee Ellen Newman of Polydor Records; Gee Records; A&M Records; Atlantic Records; MCA Records; Warner Bros. Records; Mr. and Mrs. Alan Benjamin for their 50's pictures; and Julie Kaminski for the shot of the car.